FUNDAMENTALS
OF ETHICS

by
JOHN FINNIS

Fellow of University College, Oxford

TH
II
FI-FU

GEORGETOWN UNIVERSITY PRESS
1983

Georgetown University Press,
Georgetown University,
Intercultural Center, Room 111, Washington, D.C. 20057

Copyright © 1983 by John Finnis

Library of Congress Cataloging in Publication Data
Finnis, John.
Fundamentals of ethics.
1. Ethics.   I. Title.
BJ1012.F44 1983   170   83-11693
ISBN 0-87840-404-X
ISBN 0-87840-408-2 (pbk.)

Printed in Great Britain

M.C.

R.A.   J-P.A.
C.C.G.   J.G.
M.F.

                    T.M.

Preface

These are the six Carroll Lectures (slightly revised and lightly annotated) given at Georgetown University, Washington DC, in 1982. The University and the Philosophy Department were kind hosts. I am grateful to those who helped while I was preparing the lectures, particularly to Raymond Campbell OFM Cap. and Joseph Santamaria, careful critics of early drafts. During the same period, I was able to help a little with the preparation of Germain Grisez's vast new work on fundamental moral principles; much that appears herein reflects light from that work and its predecessors.

March 1983

Contents

I. THE PRACTICALITY OF ETHICS   1
   1. Ethics is practical   1
   2. Implications of the practical character of ethics   4
   3. The great questions of ethics   6
   4. Practical understanding and nature   10
   5. 'Everyone would say . . .'   17
   6. Some conclusions about 'good' and 'nature'   20
   Notes   23

II. DESIRE, UNDERSTANDING AND HUMAN GOODS   26
   1. Reduction of ethics to (the desires of) 'human
      nature'   26
   2. Desire and understanding   30
   3. The experience machine, the critique of feelings,
      and human flourishing   37
      A. Activity has its own point   38
      B. Maintenance of one's identity is a good   39
      C. Appearances are not a good substitute for
         reality   40

   4. Is understood good the good of a system for
      securing satisfactions?   42
   5. Desire for understood goods: 'will' and
      'participation in goods'   45
   6. Thin theories of human good   48
   7. The identification of basic human goods   50
   Notes   53

III. OBJECTIVITY, TRUTH AND MORAL PRINCIPLES   56
   1. Scepticism and objectivity   56
   2. The argument from queerness   57
   3. Objectivity and truth   60
   4. From 'good' to 'right': from value judgment
      to choice   66

5. 'Right reason': the transparency of practical
    reasonableness   70
6. The variety of intermediate principles and
    the argument from relativity   74
Notes   78

IV. UTILITARIANISM, CONSEQUENTIALISM,
    PROPORTIONALISM . . . OR ETHICS?   80
    1. The varieties and the terminology   80
        A. 'Utilitarianism'   80
        B. 'Consequentialism'   82
        C. 'Teleological ethics'   84
        D. 'Proportionalism'   85
    2. Incommensurability   86
    3. How we evaluate practical solutions as 'better'
        or 'worse'   90
    4. Standard techniques of rationalization   94
    5. A new form of rationalization   99
    Notes   106

V. 'KANTIAN PRINCIPLES' AND ETHICS   109
    1. Proportionalism and the Pauline principle   109
    2. Proportionalism and Socrates' principle   112
    3. 'Treat humanity as an end, and never merely
        as a means'   120
    4. Respect every basic human good in each of your
        acts   124
    5. Can proportionalist weighing be avoided? Punish-
        ment and self-defence   127
    Notes   133

VI. ETHICS AND OUR DESTINY   136
    1. The significance of free choices   136
    2. A fundamental option to be reasonable?   142
    3. Objectivity and friendship revisited   144
    4. On 'the last things'   150
    Notes   152

INDEX   155

I
The Practicality of Ethics

I.1 *Ethics is practical*

What are we doing when we do ethics? And what is the significance of the fact that, in raising and reflecting on ethical questions, we are *doing* something?

The philosopher who may be said to have initiated, and named, the academic pursuit called *ethics* also called that pursuit 'practical'. The knowledge that one may gain by that pursuit is, he said, 'practical knowledge'. People usually water down these claims of Aristotle's. But to miss his point here is to miss not merely some truth *about* ethics as an academic pursuit. It is to miss a good opportunity of learning one of the truths *of* or *in* ethics.

The misunderstanding goes like this: Aristotle just meant that the subject-matter studied in ethics is human action (*praxis*), or opinions about human action, or opinions about right human action, or right opinions about human action, or all of these topics.

Of course, each of those topics is an aspect, more or less central, of the subject-matter of ethics. But in calling ethics practical, Aristotle had much more in mind. He meant that one does ethics properly, adequately, reasonably, if and only if one is questioning and reflecting *in order to be able to act*—i.e. in order to conduct one's life rightly, reasonably, in the fullest sense 'well'. And doubtless he had in mind that the questioning and reflecting which constitute the academic pursuit itself are themselves *actions*, the actions or conduct of you or me or Aristotle or those of his students who took his courses seriously.

This, of course, is true of all other academic and intellectual disciplines, even the most theoretical and contemplative; to choose to engage in any of them is to make some sort of a choice about how to conduct a part of one's life, the part that one devotes to that inquiry and contemplation. What then makes ethics practical?

The question must be answered carefully; if we make a mistake here we misunderstand not only ethics but also, probably, that whole range of our understanding which I am calling 'practical'. Twenty-five years ago, G. E. M. Anscombe asked: 'Can it be that there is something that modern philosophy has blankly misunderstood: namely what ancient and medieval philosophers meant by *practical knowledge?*'.[1] These twenty-five years have seen great interest in the philosophy of practical reason. This renaissance has been fruitful, but remains incomplete and insufficiently appropriated: the lure of an 'incorrigibly contemplative conception of knowledge'[2] remains strong. Now ethics *is* contemplative; indeed, it *is* theoretical (to use Aristotle's word) and speculative (to use the medieval translation of Aristotle's word, without any of the English word's connotation of 'conjectural'). That is to say, to engage in ethical inquiry and reflection is to be concerned with truth, with the right answer to one's questions, with knowledge just as such or 'for its own sake'. How, then, is ethics practical too?

Well, consider any theoretical or speculative pursuit, historical, mathematical, scientific or whatever. Anyone engaged in such pursuits, with genuinely theoretical motivation, is after a good (real or apparent) which I have already mentioned: the good of a correct or at least the most probably correct answer to his questions—if you like, the good of truth. Notice that the good envisaged and pursued has two aspects: (a) the correct answer and (b) one's obtaining it. For any theoretical inquirer, these two aspects are only formally distinct: what one wants is, compendiously, 'to get (i.e. one's getting) the right answer'. But, to the extent that one's inquiry is truly theoretical, the precise ('formal') object is the truth. When I attain it, my satisfaction may well be mixed with joy and pride that it is my own discovery, or that I am now one of those who know about the matter in question. But the primary and lasting joy of the true theorist is in the truth itself that was striven for and that now can be contemplated, both for itself and in its relation to other truths.

These facts about pure theory show themselves logically and linguistically. Let '*p*' stand for any proposition of science

[1] Anscombe, *Intention* (Blackwell, Oxford: 1957), p. 57.
[2] Id.

or history or literary criticism or common sense . . . The theorist can say to himself (1) 'I ought to think that p (since the evidence favours that conclusion)'. Or he can say (2) 'I think that p (since the evidence . . .)'. But both (1) and (2) are *transparent for* assertions that omit the first-person pronoun and its verb. That is, the meaning of (1) and of (2) can be found in assertions of the form (3) 'It is the case that [or: it's true that] p (since . . .)', or, most simply, the affirmation (3') 'p'. In formulations in form (3), the theorist—oneself as a human being with one's objective(s), one's responsibility and one's attainment—disappears from view. The logical and psychological phenomena which I call transparency will be a constant theme in these lectures on ethics (see especially III.5, V.2, VI.1, VI.3).

The reason why sentences of the form (2) 'I think . . .' are transparent (and thus completely replaceable, except as idioms for expressing uncertainty, by sentences making no use, even implicitly, of first-person terms) is the reason I have indicated already: viz., though the theorist wants to be a person who judges correctly about p, the focus of one's interest as a theorist is p, and what the proposition 'p' picks out, and the evidence for and truth of it. The focus is not *what one is doing in* considering whether p, judging that p, affirming that p . . .

And all that, save the last sentence, is true of ethics, too; for ethics is a genuinely theoretical pursuit. But ethics also is precisely and primarily ('formally') practical because the object one has in mind in doing ethics is precisely my realiz ing in my actions the *real* and *true* goods attainable by a human being and thus *my participating in* those goods. Notice: ethics is not practical merely by having as its subject-matter human action (*praxis*). Large parts of history and of psychology and of anthropology have human *praxis* as their subject-matter; but these pursuits are not practical. No: ethics is practical because my choosing and acting and living in a certain sort of way (and thus my becoming a certain sort of person: VI.1) is not a secondary (albeit inseparable and welcome) objective and side-effect of success in the intellectual enterprise; rather it is *the very objective primarily envisaged* as well as the subject-matter about which I hope to be able to affirm true propositions.

It is indeed hard to focus steadily on the fact that this academic pursuit, alone amongst all academic pursuits, has two formal, primary objects (objectives, goods in view); (i) truth about a certain subject-matter, and (ii) the instantiation of that truth in choices and actions—choices and actions of which the first, but only the first, is the investigation and affirmation of that truth (and acceptance of it as the good which discloses all the other real goods to be attained and participated in by my action).

So the temptation is powerful, and rarely resisted, to envisage ethics reductively. One reductive strategy eliminates the *radical* practicality of ethics, by envisaging ethics as a deduction from metaphysical or general anthropology (the descriptive knowledge of human nature), or as an intuition of non-natural properties of agents and actions. Another reductive strategy eliminates the theoretical, i.e. truth-seeking, character of ethics, by envisaging ethics as the expression of practical attitudes (say, 'pro-attitudes', or commitments) or states of feeling, sought to be conveyed to or impressed upon others for motives either of self-expression or of propaganda. In the latter perspective, common nowadays, the only genuinely theoretical ethics is the ('meta-ethical') study of meanings, or of communities and their languages; so this view eliminates the practical character of the study, too.

I.2   *Implications of the practical character of ethics*

But in doing ethics, one does seek truth. What one would like to know, or at least to become clearer about, is the truth about the point, the good, the worth, of human action, i.e. of one's living so far as it is constituted and shaped by one's choices. And in ethics, in the full and proper sense identified by Aristotle, one chooses to seek that truth not only 'for its own sake', nor simply for the sake of becoming a person who knows the truth about that subject-matter, but rather (and equally primarily) in order that one's choices, actions and whole way of life will be (and be known by oneself to be) good, worthwhile.

Amongst one's choices is the choice to engage in the activity of pursuing this ethical quest. It would be irrational to assert that that choice is not a good and worthwhile choice;

for like any other assertion, that assertion would need justification, and the identification of reasons for the assertion would itself be an instance of the very activity asserted to be not worthwhile. The claim that ethics is not worthwhile is either unsupported (and so not worth considering) or it is self-refuting. (What I have just said does not entail, of course, that it is not sometimes inappropriate for me to engage in ethical reflection; as we shall see, practical reasonableness requires more of one's choices than that they simply be orientated to some genuine good, however basic.)

Thus, to engage in ethical inquiry (on an appropriate occasion) is to be succeeding already, *to some extent*, in fulfilling one's fundamental intention: one's action already is a participation in an undeniable good. By one's action in engaging in ethics, one has already partially accomplished what one hoped to be able to accomplish at the end of one's inquiry and reflection. To put the point even more starkly, by one's choice to do ethics one has already made a choice of the very sort that one hoped to be able to make at the end of the perhaps long and arduous programme upon which one entered by making that choice.

Furthermore: ethics, its object, and the conditions under which that object can be attained, are properly part of the subject-matter of ethical inquiry and reflection. Ethics is genuinely reflexive. It can advance its understanding of the full human good by attending to the sort of good which leads one to engage in the pursuit of ethics. It can refute certain ethical or 'meta-ethical' claims by showing how they refute themselves; for it is explicitly aware of the intellectual commitments one makes by making any rational claim at all.

And it can advance from the study of forms of good to the study of the conditions under which those goods can reasonably be pursued; for if one is doing ethics with awareness of what one is doing, one will reflect on the conditions under which the goods directly at stake in ethical inquiry are reasonably (appropriately) pursued. One will observe, moreover, that those conditions relate not only to an assessment of appropriate and inappropriate occasions for engaging in ethical (or any other) studies, but also to an assessment of the human virtues required for any successful intellectual pursuit: truthfulness, open-mindedness, the courage to maintain open-mindedness in face of external and internal pressures and compulsions, self-discipline, and so on through a catalogue of desirable aspects of human character. Finally, since the truths to be discerned or clarified by doing ethics will concern everything that one is most deeply interested in, one may well find oneself confronting a choice between fidelity to truth (even when coming to acknowledge it will disappoint some of one's keenly felt hopes and desires) and preference for other desires and their satisfaction . . .; and the experience of confronting these open alternatives, and of choosing (say) fidelity to truth, can afford a paradigm example of free choice, and of the way in which our free choices last as virtues (or vices) and thus constitute us the particular persons we actually have come to be (VI.1).

I.3   *The great questions of ethics*

You may at this point feel some alarm. Is it being asserted that ethics is completely self-absorbed? Isn't ethics as I have been delineating it one of the last (or, remembering Aristotle, one of the first) follies of the academic mind, concerned exclusively with itself, its own objectives and pursuits, and thus wilfully (or perhaps just forgetfully) cut off from the serious business of living in a world of riches and scarcity, of sex and power, of laws, states and force?

Or again: when I've been calling ethics 'practical', haven't I been using the word in a hopelessly *unpractical* sense? And indeed, don't Aristotle's own treatises on ethics notoriously fail to confront some of the great and practical questions of morality, and even fail to give an account of practical wisdom that we could recognize as really *moral*?

These lectures are not in defence of Aristotle. Nor are they about Aristotle and his work in ethics, even though much contemporary Anglo-American moral philosophy is a debate with and about that work. I shall be saying why some of Aristotle's ethical conclusions are unsatisfactory. But the questions he worked on are real and central. For a start, take what he says about the subject-matter of ethics:

The question of the morally admirable and the question of the just— these are the subject-matter of political science [of which ethics is the primary part], and they are the subject of such variety and fluctuation that people think they are matters not of nature but of mere convention. And there is similar fluctuation of opinion about goods; for goods frequently bring harms: wealth, for example, has brought ruin to some men, and courage ruin to others.[3]

This identification of the subject-matter of ethics is often overlooked; it occurs in the midst of an academic discussion of method. And it focuses on a question which may be thought academic: Are ethical or moral judgments mere matters of convention, or are they . . .? The alternative, Aristotle formulates in terms of 'nature'. But we will understand the nub of his question better if we formulate the alternative in the modern philosophical idiom of 'objectivity'. So the question is: When we call something just, or in some other way morally admirable, are we making a judgment that can be objectively right (or wrong) and true (or false)? Or are we merely expressing, or applying, opinions adopted by individual decision and/or the conventions of our group?

The scepticism which finds its polite and conservative expression in Hume, and its radical demonic expression in Nietzsche, had been unforgettably explored by Plato and Thucydides, in the two generations before Aristotle. But there is no need to labour the point that that scepticism, in any of its forms, is not of merely academic import. It has deep practical significance for all of us. If my moral judgments are what they are just because of decisions which I or my society or civilization have consciously or unconsciously made *and could just as well have made otherwise*, the whole point of moral judgment and of action and indeed of living is put in question.

We can see this more clearly if we unpack the distinctions we have just seen Aristotle drawing between (i) good or goods [*tagatha*], (ii) the morally admirable [*to kalon*] and (iii) the just [*to dikaion*]. A great deal of ethics has to do with justice. But not as much as many people now think. Once we have determined what it is wrong to do to other people, or not to do for other people, there remains the question attributed to Socrates in the *Apology* and again in the *Gorgias* and, most elaborately, in the *Republic*: Is it

[3] *Nic. Eth.* I. 3: 1097b14-17.

better to suffer wrong than to do it? That question, as we shall see (V.2) is a challenge to all forms of utilitarianism or consequentialism or proportionalism. But it is not really a question about the content of justice, i.e. about what is right and wrong in dealings with other people. Nor, indeed, is it about what choices are right and what are wrong in any other context. Rather, the question concerns the whole *point* of moral thought and life.

The great question raised and wrestled with by Plato in the *Republic* is 'What is the good of living justly, morally, uprightly?' That sense of 'good', more fundamental than 'moral good' (though not perhaps than *to kalon*, which is not as narrow or specific as our term 'moral good'), is the sense of the comparative, 'better', in the Socratic–Platonic affirmation: 'It is better to suffer wrong than to do it'. It is also the 'good' in the similar question foreshadowed by Aristotle in the passage I quoted: 'What is the good of courage if it can bring me to ruin and death?' And it is the good or complex of goods which Aristotle says his ethics is in pursuit of—and remember, that pursuit will be successful if and only if one not only discovers the truth about that good but also in some measure participates in that good.

In its fullness, that good or complex of goods is called by Aristotle *eudaimonia*, 'happiness' or, better translated, *flourishing*. But that sort of good, as Aristotle thinks, is worth participating in (by *eupraxia*, goodness of action, that part of *eudaimonia* which is a matter of one's choice rather than one's good- or ill-fortune) even when, by ill-fortune, it is not available in its fullness: when, for example, doing justice takes courage because it will cause one suffering. Or (we may add) when I am out of range of the problems of justice, alone on a desert island without prospect of rescue, and the question is 'Shall I spend the rest of my time submerged in the pleasures of drug-induced fantasy and solitary sex?'

Now these, you can see, are truly practical questions. Once they have been raised they cannot be put back into the bottle by appeals to the custom of the tribe, the values of our civilization, or even the sheer commands of the deity. Each one of us may have to sacrifice his interests for the sake of justice: What is the good of that? (and don't try to tell me just that it may work in my interests in the long run; if that's all that's at stake, I'd be willing to take a chance on looking after my own long-term interests by my own cunning and ruthlessness, and so I'd do without the sacrifice now being asked of me). And again, each one of us is to some extent outside the range of justice, alone on one's individual island of existence and experience and facing the question whether the point of one's individual existence is experiences of an agreeable sort: gratifications, satisfactions . . .

The great questions of ethics can be approached in many ways. Here are three peculiarly strategic questions:

(1) The question of justice and the limits of its claims upon us as individuals or communities. It has many aspects; one of its most acute forms is the famous question put on the lips of Caiaphas:[4] *'Is it not better that one innocent person be put to death than that the whole people perish?'*.

(2) That first question can still be interpreted as a question about the content of justice: utilitarians or consequentialists, who provide rationalizations for pragmatists (IV.4), will answer: 'It is right, i.e. in accordance with justice all things considered, that one man should die rather than many'. So the second great question sharpens the point for those of us who are inclined to think that that utilitarian answer, whatever else may be said for it, is certainly not in accordance with justice, and that the innocent man thus put to death has been wronged. For those of us who think thus, the question arises in the form posed and answered by Socrates (see V.2 below): *Is it better to do wrong or to suffer it? How could it be?*

(3) The sense of the term 'better' (and thus of the implicit term 'good') in the two preceding questions can be directly explored by setting aside the problem of our relations to each other and simply asking: *Am I to live just for agreeable experiences?*

Those are three practical questions which, in one variant or another, are fundamental to ethical inquiry. The principles which become apparent in considering them will determine the method of answering all other practical questions, and in that way will determine the whole content of ethics.

[4] Cf. *John* 11: 50; 18: 14.

Precisely because they are practical (i.e. about *what to do*), those three questions provide the authentic context for discussing the two academic methodological issues which dominate contemporary ethical theorizing. If you wish, you can regard these two issues as the academic themes of this book. They are (1) the issue of *objectivity* and scepticism, treated in the next two chapters; and (2) the issue of utilitarianism or consequentialism or *proportionalism*, discussed in the fourth and fifth chapters. (The sixth chapter examines the reality of free choice, and the way one's choices create not only the transitive effects which proportionalists offer to sum and weigh but also, intransitively, one's character and thus one's destiny.)

I.4   *Practical understanding and nature*

Why do I emphasize the fact (or, if you prefer, the Aristotelian thesis) that the understanding we seek and attain in ethics is *practical*? And didn't I fudge an important and notorious problem when discussing Aristotle's description of the subject-matter of ethics? For while Aristotle said that some think the good and the right are matters merely of convention [or decision], not *of nature*, I rendered that as: 'matters merely of decision and convention, not *objective*'. In replacing the word 'nature' with the word 'objective', wasn't I shuffling out of sight the claim of classical ethics to be founded on *nature* and on a true metaphysics or descriptive knowledge of nature—the claim which to some is the chief merit and to others the all-vitiating fallacy of pre-Enlightenment ethical theories?

The question how practical understanding relates to our knowledge of nature (especially human nature as known in a general [metaphysical or other descriptive] anthropology) provides a useful opening into the discussion of ethical objectivity. Moreover, some have thought the title of my book *Natural Law and Natural Rights* a misdescription, in view of my theses about the relation of 'is'-judgments to 'ought'-judgments. So I shall devote the rest of this chapter to sorting out this delicate academic issue.

I begin with two warnings. Do not be misled by Aristotle's talk of two 'parts' of the intellect, the theoretical and the practical; or by Aristotelian and Thomistic talk about 'the theoretical intellect and the practical intellect'. Despite these ways of talking, Aristotle and Aquinas were well enough aware that each of us has only one intelligence, only one capacity (power, ability . . .) of understanding. So the differences between 'theoretical' and 'practical' understanding are simply operational differences. And there are these differences between one's intellectual operations simply because there is a difference of objectives. One is thinking theoretically (i.e. 'speculatively', which need not mean conjecturally) when one is concerned primarily with discerning the truth about some topic. One is thinking practically when one is concerned primarily to discover or determine what to do, to get, to have or to be. I have already tried (I.1) to illustrate this difference of objectives.

The second warning follows on immediately. Each of the terms 'theoretical' and 'practical' is obviously an analogous term, i.e. a term whose meaning shifts systematically as one uses it.[5] While there are no doubt paradigm cases of purely theoretical and purely practical intellectual activity, most of our actual thinking is *both* theoretical (at least in some qualified sense) *and* practical. Much of the time we are to some extent interested in the truth just 'for its own sake' *and* to some extent interested in it because we want to get it (and be the sort of person who has it). And very often we are interested in the truth only because, being concerned about something else (living a good life, or treating a friend rightly, or staying healthy, or finding the best candidate or the cheapest coffee . . .), we want that concern to be intelligent and well-informed.

Bearing both those warnings in mind, I shall say that one is thinking practically, or exercising practical understanding, when one is considering what to be, to get, to have or to do. And that can also be expressed as follows, using the term 'good' in that informal, idiomatic sense which is not tied to

---

[5] That is to say, one uses the term not only (as the medievals put it) *simpliciter*, i.e. in an unqualified way, to refer to 'central' or 'paradigmatic' instances. One uses the term also to refer to instances which significantly have some but lack others of the features of the central or paradigmatic instances; these secondary, more or less borderline uses of any term the medievals called *secundum quid*, and modern philosophy has not come up with a better jargon: 'qualified' seems the nearest equivalent.

'morality': one is thinking practically, or exercising practical understanding, when one is considering what it is (or would be, under relevantly possible conditions) good to be, to get, to have or to do. Such thinking or understanding is practical *simpliciter* [without qualification] when my consideration is of my own predicament with a view to undertaking my own commitments and/or actions here and now. It is practical *secundum quid* [in a qualified sense] (but still primarily practical rather than theoretical) when my consideration is more reflective, reviewing my present commitments and past actions, contemplating future commitments and actions, or assessing the commitments, actions and characters of other persons . . .

My thesis, then, is this: one's primary understanding of human good, and of what it is worthwhile for human beings to seek to do, to get, to have and to be, is attained when one is considering what it would be good, worthwhile to do, to get, to have and to be—i.e., by definition, when one is thinking practically. My thesis does not for a moment deny that the understanding thus attained can be integrated into a general account of human nature, i.e. of human potentialities and their various forms of fulfilment. What I do assert is that our primary grasp of what is good for us (or: really a fulfilment of our potentialities) is a practical grasp.

Aristotle and Aquinas, I believe, both accepted the thesis I have just put forward. Misunderstandings, however, arise for various reasons which are important for the history of philosophy, and indeed for an account of the self-understanding of everyone involved in the western civilization whose common speech has been so profoundly formed by Aristotle. I may mention four of these reasons for misunderstanding.

(i) Aristotle was deeply interested in an anthropology continuous on the one side with his biology and on the other side with his cosmology and theology. (ii) Aquinas the theologian was likewise interested in pointing out the analogies running through the whole order of being, for instance the analogy of virtue whereby human virtue is analogous to the the virtue that can be predicated of anything which is a fine specimen of things of its nature (i.e. things of that sort . . .). (iii) The followers of Aristotle and of Aquinas, more interested in systematizing the results of their respective master's investigations than in retracing those investigations, sub-scribed to drastic simplifications of the method of those investigations; in short, they commonly misread their masters' epistemology. And finally (iv) Aristotle himself launched at least one argument which uses or presupposes a mistaken view of the way that judgments about nature can contribute to understanding in ethics.

Let me, at last, give an example. Aristotle's *Nicomachean Ethics* is fundamentally an attempt to identify (in order to participate in) the true good and point of human existence. (He supposes that to identify such an ultimate good is to supply a 'grand universal premise'[6] for all practical thinking and thus for all reasonable action.) What does the ultimate or supreme good consist in? What, to give it a name, does *eudaimonia* ('happiness' or, better, 'flourishing') consist in? Notoriously, Aristotle's answer has been found obscure, equivocal and in various ways unconvincing. But my present concern is not with his answer but with his method.

I shall begin with the accounts given by two contemporary Aristotelians. Sympathetic, critical and sensitive philosophical discussion of Aristotle's ethics is readily available today, and quite a few modern moral philosophers are clearly influenced by Aristotle, and not ashamed to admit it; begin the list with John Rawls. But not many would describe themselves as Aristotelians. Let me consider two who do, Mortimer Adler and Henry Veatch.

Adler[7] enthusiastically endorses the following conception of practical truth, a conception which is, he says, Aristotle's. With one exception, a practical or normative judgment is true if and only if it agrees with 'right desire'; the exception is 'the one self-evident principle that lies at the foundation of all moral reasoning', namely the principle that 'real goods ought to be desired'. Now, if you ask what makes a desire right, or a good a real good, Adler's answer is in each case the same: a desire is right when it is for a real good, and a good is a real good when it is the object of a desire that is not

---

[6] G. E. M. Anscombe, 'Thought and Action in Aristotle: What is Practical Truth?' in *Collected Philosophical Papers of G. E. M. Anscombe*, vol. I (Blackwell, Oxford: 1981), p. 75.

[7] Adler, 'Aristotle's Conception of Practical Truth and the Consequences of that Conception', *Paideia* (SUNY at Brockport), Special Aristotle Issue, 1978, pp. 158-66.

a mere want but a *need*. A need is, says Adler, a desire that is natural, i.e. 'inherent in our common human nature'. The judgment that a desire is natural is a purely 'descriptive or factual proposition': in Humean or neo-Humean terms it is an 'is' not an 'ought'. Thus, for instance, the judgment 'I ought to seek knowledge' is the conclusion of a piece of practical reasoning in which the first premise is the normative principle 'Real goods ought to be desired' and the second premise is the factual truth that 'Man has a natural desire for knowledge'; being a conclusion from these two truths, the one factual but the other normative, the judgment 'I ought to seek knowledge' is a practical truth.[8] Thus Adler.

Now Aristotle's term for the 'descriptive and factual' as opposed to the 'normative' is *theoretikē* (as opposed to *praktikē*). How, then, could the crucial 'factual' premises of Adler's practical syllogisms be the topic of an ethics which Aristotle says is *practical all the way through*? Adler himself frankly admits that in the very place where Aristotle mentions a large number of particular goods, viz. in Book I of the *Nicomachean Ethics*, one 'cannot find . . . any reference, however slight, to the appetitive tendencies that are inherent in human nature, much less an inventory of man's natural appetites that would enable us to ascertain the real goods at which they aim'.[9] Quite so. The fact is that Aristotle is not a neo-Aristotelian who believes that ethical truths are attained by an inventory (or any other description) of aspects of human nature.

Henry Veatch, on the other hand, does not seek an inventory of the 'real goods'. But he does think that Aristotelian ethics turns on an identification of *the* good, the supreme good, of human life. And that identification, he insists, is made not in the ethics (which is a practical science) but in the physics, the great Aristotelian inquiry into the natures of the various kinds of substances in the natural world, including human nature. Ethics begins only *after* we 'as physicists'[10] have identified the *telos* of human development.

Admirably clear. But rather mysterious, given that Aristotle's own inquiry into the *telos* of human existence is *the*

---

[8] Adler, op. cit., pp. 161-3.   [9] Ibid., p. 164.
[10] Henry Veatch, *Aristotle: a Contemporary Appreciation* (Indiana UP, Bloomington and London: 1974), p. 99.

subject-matter of the *Ethics*, notably Books I and X, in each of which Aristotle insists that what he is doing is practical, not theoretical.

I hasten to add that there is in the *Nicomachean Ethics* an argument of Aristotle's that has something of the 'theoretical', i.e. non-practical, character which Adler and Veatch make decisive for ethics. It occurs as one part of the famous argument about man's *ergon*, function or characteristic activity: *Nic. Eth.* I, 7: 1097b24-1098a20. (Veatch says that this argument is for Aristotle 'the way' to identify true *eudaimonia*; but in fact it is only one of many arguments employed by Aristotle in his search for that identification.) Aristotle's concern to identify the human function is treated with much more sympathy by contemporary philosophers than it was by the philosophers of the last few generations. But there is one part of it which is rightly found unacceptable, and that is the very part or moment which is unequivocally 'theoretical', non-practical; for the rest of the argument can be construed either as theoretical (as it is by Adler and Veatch) or as practical. The one purely theoretical moment of the argument is where Aristotle says we should be looking not merely for man's function or characteristic activity but, more narrowly, for man's *peculiar* characteristic activity, i.e. the function he does not share with any other being.

Life seems to belong even to plants, but we are seeking what is peculiar to man. Let us exclude, therefore, the life of nutrition and growth. Next there would be the life of perception, but *it* also seems to be shared even by the horse, the ox, and every animal. There remains, then . . .[11]

And so on.

But, *pace* Aristotle, we should not suppose that the most important characteristics of humanity are to be identified by identifying those that distinguish us from all other kinds of being. For one thing, the argument would lead to a conclusion which Aristotle does not want; for he wants all his arguments to support his view that the ultimate *telos* of man is *theoretical* contemplation; but contemplation is not peculiar to human beings; it is a characteristic which, on Aristotle's own account, we share with the gods. But the

[11] *Nic. Eth.* I, 7: 1097b34-1098a3 (trans. Ross).

main thing wrong with Aristotle's 'unique function' argument is simply that it adduces a bare fact (the alleged fact that we are unique in such and such a respect). Though this may be a fact of great significance for a description of the universe, it has no significance for practical understanding, i.e. for an understanding of what is *good* in human life. The argument is a piece of bare 'physics', from which nothing of this sort follows for ethics.

Indeed, Henry Veatch gives silent, perhaps unwilling, testimony in support of my objection. For, having quoted Aristotle's function argument, with its conclusion (as Veatch renders it) that the unique function and, therefore, ultimate goal of human life is 'the practical life of the rational part of man', he gives what amounts to his own argument for that conclusion. Remember, on Veatch's own account of method, this argument should be a piece of physics, of theoretical and not practical reasoning. You will observe how different it in fact is, and how much better it is for being different, i.e. for being practical, i.e. directly concerned with the good and the reasonable:

(1) . . . man's function, or man's perfection or full-development, does indeed consist in . . . his living in the manner of someone with knowledge and understanding, and (2) . . . it is just this end that all men do strive for and that is consequently the source of their true happiness and satisfaction. For as regards (1), *would we not all acknowledge that* however healthy or fully developed a human being might be in a narrowly physical or biological sense, and however well he might be provided for in his ordinary needs and desires, if in general he acted and behaved in a way that was no better than a fool, we should hardly say that such a person's existence was quite what we would consider to be a full or proper existence for a human being. Similarly, as regards (2), *imagine yourself in a situation where you* would be offered all of the usual and perhaps unusual necessities and even goods of life . . . but at the price of . . . not having any genuine knowledge or understanding either of yourself or of the nature of things generally—that is to say, at the price of your not asking any questions . . . and so of your not really knowing the what or the why of anything. *Would you settle for this?* Presumably not. But, then, is not Aristotle right in his insistence that the good or final cause of human life is precisely the intelligent life . . .?[12]

The argument appeared to set out, unpromisingly, by asking what 'all men do strive for', an ethically barren question of

---

[12] Op. cit., pp. 106-7, emphases added.

'physics'. And the question what is a 'full and proper existence for a human being' seemed to be being asked in a
purely theoretical way. But as the argument unfolds, we can
see that it *works*, i.e. induces understanding and knowledge
of what is a full and proper human existence, precisely by
getting you to 'imagine yourself in a situation where you
would be . . .', and asking 'Would you settle for this?'

True, the argument gets you to acknowledge something
which can indeed be expressed in a proposition about human
nature. But it does this by getting you to consider a question
which, though hypothetical, is none the less practical. (For
the argument would work *in just the same way* if the question
were not hypothetical but required of you a choice here and
now between the alternative lives (forms of life); thus its
being hypothetical does not remove its radically practical
character.) Bare facts about the natural order, such as that all
men do strive for such-and-such, and/or that strivings for that
are peculiar to human beings, play no part whatsoever in this
argument of Veatch's.

I.5 *'Everyone would say . . .'*

Nor, usually, do such facts about the natural order play a role
in Aristotle's argument. As Adler had to admit, appeals to
what is natural or universal or peculiar to one species are
virtually absent from the *Ethics*. The 'function' argument is
not the deep structure of Aristotle's ethical method; it is an
erratic boulder. The whole argument of the *Ethics* concludes
to a proposition about what is natural to man, in the sense of
truly appropriate to and fulfilling for human beings; but that
is the conclusion, or a way of expressing the conclusion, and
the arguments for it are found elsewhere. Where?

Time and again Aristotle appeals to what 'everyone would
say', or 'no one would say', or 'everyone (or no one . . .)
would choose'. These appeals are not at all to be understood
as claiming or presupposing that philosophical opinions are
to be accepted or rejected according as they enjoy the
support of the majority or the multitude; on the contrary,
Aristotle says time and again that on questions such as 'What

is the good for man?' we do not have to defer to the opinions of the multitude.[13]

Still less is the ultimate goal of ethical inquiry an understanding of 'the structure of moral language', as some modern philosophers of ethics (or meta-ethics) would have it. No, the goal of ethical inquiry is identification of and participation in the true human good. The primary and, in my view, the proper function of those appeals to what we or others (or 'everyone') would say or choose is to *prompt* or *remind* us (the present participants in the inquiry) firstly, of our own and others' pre-philosophical experience, and secondly, of our own and others' practical and pre-philosophical grasp of good(s).

'We ought to attend to the undemonstrated sayings and opinions of experienced and older people not less than to demonstrations; for because experience has given them an eye they see aright'.[14] And that just appreciation of the human situation is to be found crystallized in the language of praise and blame. But you and I, doing ethics, need to *appropriate* that just appreciation of the human situation. We make that appropriation, not by parrotting common opinions, nor by appeals to the fact that most people agree with the opinion we are espousing, but by attending to precisely those aspects of our experience (or of the experience of others which their testimony makes accessible to us) of which our language serves as a reminder and in which human good(s) became or can now become intelligible to us.

The decisive moves in Aristotle's argument identifying the ultimate good(s) of human life are moves like these:

No one would choose to live with the intellect of a child throughout his life, however much he were to be pleased at the things that children are pleased at . . .[15]

(Observe that this is the principle tacitly appealed to, or exemplified, by the convincing part of Veatch's argument concerning the good of intelligent living. Indeed, in a parallel version of his argument to identify 'man's *telos*', Veatch makes the move explicitly and to clinch his argument: 'by

[13] *Nic. Eth.* I, 4: 1095a22; 5: 1095b14-22; *Eud. Eth.* I, 4: 1214b35.
[14] *Nic. Eth.* VI, 11: 1143b12-14.
[15] *Nic. Eth.* X, 3: 1174a1-3; see also 6: 1176b22-3; *Eud. Eth.* I, 5: 1215b23-4.

and large no man in his senses would prefer the existence of a contented cow . . . to the existence of a human being with at least some understanding of what is going on'—for such understanding, or even the semblance of it, 'means more to a human being than anything else'.[16] We shall meet this contention again when we experiment in thought with the 'experience machine': II.3.)

No-one chooses to possess the whole world if he has first to become someone else . . .; he wishes for this only on condition of being whatever he is . . .[17]

(This, too, we shall explore further in the context of the experience machine.)

No-one would choose the whole world on condition of being alone . . .[18]
No-one chooses *eudaimonia* for the sake of honour, pleasure, etc., nor as a means to anything whatever other than itself[19]

And so on.

In each case, the 'no one would . . .' is a reminder of human experience, including the experience (actual or vicarious) of Aristotle's own reader, you or me. It is a reminder too, of a pre-philosophic understanding of that experience, including notably the reader's own previous understanding. So the appeal is not to numbers. Nor, on the other hand, is it a mere dogmatic begging of the question. For the opinions in question are not recalled as being philosophical answers to the philosophical question in issue (the question of the true human good(s)). Rather, they are recalled as expressing an understanding of particular aspects of the matter—as a set of insights which, when recalled, assembled and brought to bear on the question, will help to justify a thesis that is philosophical not by being less practical but by being more *general*, more *systematic* in relating each relevant proposition to all the others, and thus, above all, more *explanatory*.

[16] Henry Veatch, *Rational Man: a Modern Interpretation of Aristotelian Ethics* (Indiana UP, Bloomington and London: 1962), pp. 56-7.
[17] *Nic. Eth.* IX, 4: 1166a19–22.
[18] *Nic. Eth.* IX, 9: 1169b17 (trans. Ross). There are some doubts about the authenticity and proper translation of this passage. But see also VIII, 7: 1159a9–11.
[19] *Nic. Eth.* I, 7: 1097b6.

I.6 *Some conclusions about 'good' and 'nature'*

Aristotle's effort was to identify and participate in that form (or set of forms) of human life that is really and supremely good, desirable, preferable—even if it turns out to be one which, if luck is against us, may involve us in suffering. And that effort should be ours, too, in doing ethics.

Now any thesis about what is in this sense supremely good for you or me, or any other human being, can helpfully be expressed in various sorts of ways. It can be expressed as a thesis about what a human being should do or be; or what it is the business (not necessarily the *peculiar* function) of a human being to do or be; or what fulfils a human being; or what fully actualizes the potentialities of human nature; or what is in keeping with human nature . . . These last formulae, referring explicitly to human nature, can thus be a way of expressing the conclusions of an openly evaluative, practical, ethical investigation. Such references to what is (humanly) natural *need* not be regarded as an appeal to, or expression of, some independent, 'value-free' investigation of the sort that Veatch would call (Aristotelian) physics, and that we might call general anthropology.

On the other hand, while agreeing with John McDowell in that conclusion, I cannot agree with him that 'such an explicit mention of human nature would be a sort of rhetorical flourish, added to a conclusion already complete without it.'[20] There is a legitimate, theoretical (non-practical) investigation and description of human nature, and it cannot be a satisfactory description unless it incorporates results *which cannot be obtained except by that practical pursuit that Aristotle called ethics.* In our theoretical descriptions of the nature of other types of beings, we have to be content with what we can discover by the use of rather 'external' techniques; and those techniques will doubtless tell us much about human beings, too. But why suppose that our techniques for developing a description of *human* nature are limited to those available for describing beings whose nature we do not share?

[20] McDowell, 'The Role of *Eudaimonia* in Aristotle's Ethics', in Amélie Rorty (ed.), *Essays on Aristotle's Ethics* (U. California P., Berkeley, Los Angeles, London: 1980), p. 371 (cf. p. 375 n. 27).

As I have said, Aristotle did not suppose so. His only treatises on human nature are his *Ethics* and his *Politics*, i.e. his practical and unequivocally evaluative 'philosophy of human matters [*ta anthrōpina*], complete as far as possible'[21] And this is no literary accident. For a study of the nature of a being is, for Aristotle, a study of the potentialities or capacities of that being. And Aristotle has a methodological principle which contradicts Adler's view that human goods are to be understood by reference to an inventory of 'inherent' human desires. The order of explanatory understanding, for Aristotle, is just the opposite: potentialities or capacities are understood by understanding their corresponding acts (actualizations); and acts or actualizations are in turn to be understood by understanding their objects.[22] Now the principal *objects* of human life (i.e. of our capacities and our activities) are precisely the concern of practical reason, i.e. of our thinking about what to do and be. They are the subject-matter of that disciplined inquiry which Aristotle named ethics, an inquiry which one pursues, if one pursues it fully, not merely to find out about a topic (human good, i.e. the forms of human flourishing), but to realize and participate in those object(ive)s, those forms of human flourishing, with all one's being, by all one's choices and dispositions.

In the 'ontological order', no doubt, 'the essence of the soul grounds the potencies, the potencies ground the acts, and the acts ground knowledge of objects'.[23] But if you ask how we come to know human essence or nature, the order will be that stated by Aristotle himself: one must first know the objects, and thus one can fully know the characteristic human acts, and *thus* the human potentialities, and *thus* the human essence or nature. And the object(ive)s of human acts are the intelligible goods that make sense to someone choosing what to do . . .

Epistemologically, (knowledge of) human nature is not 'the basis of ethics'; rather, ethics is an indispensable preliminary to a full and soundly based knowledge of human nature. What one can and should say about human nature,

---

[21] *Nic. Eth.* X, 9: 1181b15.
[22] *De Anima* II, 4: 415a16-21. See also Aquinas, *Summa Theologiae* I, q. 87, a. 3c; *in II De Anima*, lect. 6, nn. 304-8; *in III De Anima*, lect. 9, n. 803.
[23] Bernard Lonergan, *Collection* (Herder, New York: 1967), p. 153.

as the result of one's ethical inquiries, is not mere rhetorical addition; it finds a place in the sober and factual account of what it is to be a human being.

I am not for a moment saying that everything that we know about human nature comes from our ethical under-standing. Nor am I saying that our ethical understanding can be acquired independently of all 'factual', descriptive, 'theoretical' knowledge; I am not proposing a kind of ethical 'intuitionism' . . . As I have said elsewhere:

> There is thus a mutual though not quite symmetrical *interdependence* between the project of describing human affairs by way of theory and the project of evaluating human options with a view, at least remotely, to acting reasonably and well. The evaluations are in no way deduced from the descriptions . . .; but one whose knowledge of the facts of the human situation is very limited is unlikely to judge well in discerning the practical implications of the basic values [which indeed cannot be grasped at all without a knowledge of possibilities]. Equally, the descriptions are not deduced from the evaluations; but without the evaluations one cannot determine what descriptions are really illuminat-ing and significant.[24]

Ethics is not deduced or inferred from metaphysics or anthropology. But a mistaken metaphysics or anthropology will block one's reflective understanding of the way in which one participates in the human goods (particularly the good of practical reasonableness itself). If, for example, one supposes that reason is the slave of the passions, a mere instrument for efficiently sorting out and attaining wants that are simply given prior to all understanding (II.1-3), one will find no reason to give the requirements of practical reasonableness (III.4-6) their architectonic and conclusive force.

I have been exploring what Aristotle could have had in mind when he raised, as a central concern of ethics, the question whether the just, the right, the good, are matters of convention only or *physei*, grounded in *nature* (I.3 above). That should be construed, I said, as raising the question of the *objectivity* of ethical judgments.

That question is now still more urgent. For everything I have been saying supposes that the judgments about human good(s) and the truly worthwhile objects of human existence

---

[24] Finnis, *Natural Law and Natural Rights* (Clarendon Press, Oxford: 1980), abbreviated *NLNR*, below, p. 19; the bracketed insertion is from p. 77.

are objective judgments, judgments capable of being true
regardless of our decisions or the conventions of our language
or the customs of our communities. And I have not yet said
much to show how our opinions about human good(s) need
not be the slave of our desires, or of the desires embodied in
the conventions of our culture. In the next chapter, I try to
show just that. That will also help to show what the human
good(s) consist in, and will begin my response to the three
great questions of conduct (I.3), particularly the third: Am I
to live just for agreeable experiences?

NOTES

I.1

Ethics, properly done, is done in order to act well . . . See Aristotle,
Nic. Eth. I, 3: 1095a6; II, 1: 1103b27-9; X, 8: 1179a35-b4; read with
VI, 4: 1140b3-6 ('in doing . . ., goodness of action [*eupraxia*] is in
itself the goal'), and *Pol.* VII, 3: 1325b14-21. Also *Meta.* II, 1: 993b21;
Eud. Eth. I, 5: 1216b19-25. Also John M. Cooper, *Reason and Human
Good in Aristotle* (Harvard UP, Cambridge, Mass. and London: 1975),
pp. 71, 111 (but the explication in n. 98 on p. 71 is not strong enough).

Transparency . . . See Roy Edgley, *Reason in Theory and Practice*
(Hutchinson, London: 1969), p. 97 ('my own present thinking, in contrast to the thinking of others, is transparent in the sense that I cannot
distinguish the question "Do I think that *p*?" from a question in which
there is no essential reference to myself or my belief, namely "Is it the
case that *p*?"', etc.); also pp. 127-30 (e.g. 'when someone is thinking
or wondering whether to do *x*, the same transparency holds (and
indeed, thinking that the thing to do is *x* is one form of thinking that *p*)
. . . No one can distinguish his own question of what to do from his
own question of what answer to give to that question', etc.). Expressions in the first person have special features, many of which are
explored by G. E. M. Anscombe in defending her stark thesis that 'I'
is not a name and is not an expression which *refers* at all: 'The First
Person' in her *Collected Philosophical Papers*, vol. II, *Metaphysics and
the Philosophy of Mind* (Blackwell, Oxford: 1981), pp. 21-36. See
III.5 below.

I.2

'Ethics is not worthwhile' is a self-refuting assertion . . . See Finnis,
NLNR, pp. 73-5, 79-80.

I.3

When Aristotle contrasts 'by convention' with 'by nature', the latter phrase connotes 'objectively' . . . 'By nature' (*physei*) is a phrase with many connotations, but in this context the reference to objectivity or truth is uppermost; *Nic. Eth.* I, 3: 1094b14–17 looks forward to V, 7: 1134b18–1135a15, where the key affirmations are (i) 'a rule of justice is natural that has the same validity everywhere and does not depend on our accepting it or not' (1134b20); and (ii) 'in all places there is only one political order (*politeia*) that is natural, namely, the best' (1135a5). But the question which is the best *politeia* is a question with answers that are right or wrong, true or false: see *Pol.* VII, 1: 1323a14–16; VII, 2: 1324a23–33. And, in general, the discerning and establishing of justice is the work of *phronesis* (*Nic. Eth.* VI, 8: 1141b23 ff.), and *phronesis* is a '*truth*-attaining rational quality concerned with action in relation to things that are good and bad for human beings' (VI, 5: 1140b6–8). For a very suggestive commentary, see the essays 'What is Right by Nature?' and 'What is Nature?' in Eric Voegelin, *Anamnesis* (University of Notre Dame Press, Notre Dame and London: 1978).

I.4

Ethics is practical all the way through . . . See Aquinas's commentaries on Aristotle, *in Pol.* proem. nn. 5, 6, 7, 8; *in Eth.* II, lect. 2 (n. 256), lect. 9 (n. 351). Correspondingly, the basic methodological principle in Aristotle's treatises on ethics and politics is that, in these matters, 'things really are what they appear to be to the *spoudaios*' [the *virtuosus* in Aquinas's Latin, i.e. the person of *practical* wisdom]: *Nic. Eth.* III, 4: 1113a23–b1; X, 5: 1176a16–17. See also Finnis, *NLNR*, pp. 15n, 31, 101–3, 128–9, 366 at n. 25.

I.5

The 'function' argument is an erratic boulder in the Ethics . . . The argument from peculiarity is found more than once. At the end of the function argument in Book I, 7, Aristotle launches onto the 'digression' about virtues, which will occupy Books I–IX (the announced reason for the digression being that if the function of man is rational activity, the function of a good man will be the good, noble, excellent, i.e. in short the virtuous performance of such activity). But at the end of the digression will be found the famous (though still by no means the only) argument of Book X, that 'If happiness is activity, it is reasonable that it should be in accordance with the highest virtue and this highest virtue will be that of the best thing in us', and the eighth of the eight arguments Aristotle adduces to identify the contemplative exercise of reason as the best life is the peculiarity argument: 'that which is proper to each thing is by nature best and pleasantest for each thing; for man, therefore, the life according to reason is best and pleasantest, since reason more than anything else *is* man': *Nic. Eth.* X, 7: 1177a12–13, 1178a7–8.

Arguments from 'what everyone would say . . .' as reminders of experience and pre-philosophical understanding . . . See J. Donald Monan, *Moral Knowledge and its Methodology in Aristotle* (OUP: 1968), pp. 96–106.

I.6

We come to understand acts by understanding their objects, and capacities by understanding their act(uation)s . . . This principle, stated in *De Anima* II, 4: 415a17-23, is foreshadowed by Aristotle in I, 1: 402b15. It is vigorously expressed and extended (in conformity with Aristotle's intentions) by Aquinas in his commentary: 'ut per objecta cognoscamus actus, et per actus potentias, et per potentias essentiam animae'. By knowing a being's potentialities you know its essence or nature; but you know those capacities by knowing their actuations, and you know or understand those actualizations by understanding what objects (in Latin *objecta*, in Greek *antikeimena*) are thereby attained —i.e. known, if it is a question of the act of knowing; realized, if it is a question of willing, doing, making . . . Aquinas employs and uses this principle from his earliest to his latest works. *Objectum* can refer to many types of thing: anything that can come in the direct-object place after a finite or transitive verb can be called an object: see Anthony Kenny in Aquinas, *Summa Theologiae*, Blackfriars edn, vol. 22 (London and New York: 1964), p. 100n; also pp. 96n, 118, 135. (For the emergence of the word *objectum* and thus of the similar English word we now use to translate *antikeimenon*, see L. Dewan, ' "Obiectum": Notes on the Invention of a Word' (1981) 48 *Archives d'Histoire Doctrinale et Littéraire du Moyen Age*, 37-96, esp. pp. 64-78, 91, 93-4).

The object of the human will is goods under the aspect of 'good' . . . See Finnis, *NLNR*, chs. III, IV. According to Aquinas, the object of the will is 'bonum et finis in communi' (*ST* I, q. 82, a. 4c), 'bonum apprehensum' (*de Ver.* 22, 9 ad 6), 'bonum intellectum' (*ST* I, q. 21, a. 1 ad 2), 'bonum secundum rationem' (*ST* I, q. 59, a. 4c)—what I call general forms of good, referred to by desirability characterizations. Aquinas offers a basic inventory of these in *ST* I-II, q. 94, a. 2c and earlier, in a fragmentary form, in *ST* I-II, q. 10, a. 1c, where he mentions 'truth and life, etc.', having pointed out that these 'comprehenduntur sub objecto voluntatis, sicut quaedam particularia bona' since 'homo naturaliter vult non solum objectum voluntatis, sed etiam alia quae conveniunt aliis potentiis'.

II
Desire, Understanding and Human Goods

II.1 Reduction of ethics to (the desires of) 'human nature'

There is nothing truly good or bad, right or wrong; if there is to be an ethics, we must 'invent' those categories. In asserting this, John Mackie rightly counted himself an authentic successor of Hobbes and Hume. (We have seen that there were thinkers known to Plato and Aristotle who had passed that way before: I.3.) As Mackie says:

> We can take Thomas Hobbes as the first speaker in a sustained philosophical debate that . . . culminates in, but does not end with, Hume's moral theory. . . . [For Hobbes] 'good' and 'evil' are words which express only the relation of things to the speaker's desires.
>
> Whatsoever is the object of any man's appetite or desire, that is it which he for his part calleth *good*: and the object of his hate, and aversion, *evil*; and of his contempt, *vile* and *inconsiderable*. For these words of good, evil, and contemptible, are ever used with relation to the person that useth them: there being nothing simply and absolutely so; nor any common rule of good and evil, to be taken from the nature of the objects themselves . . .
>
> There is no room for objective moral qualities or relations. . . .
>
> the main outlines of [Hobbes's] theory still stand. He was right in denying objective moral qualities and relations.[1]

For one who takes this view, 'the foundation of ethics' (Hume's phrase) will be 'the particular fabric and constitution of the human species'.[2] Such an author will offer us, like Hobbes, a treatise *De Homine*, or like Hume, a *Treatise of*

---

[1] J. L. Mackie, *Hume's Moral Theory* (Routledge & Kegan Paul, London and Boston: 1980), pp. 7, 150; the internal quotation is from Hobbes, *Leviathan* (1651), ch. VI (Raphael, *British Moralists*, para. 25).

[2] Hume, *An Enquiry concerning the Principles of Morals* ([1751], 1777), sec. I (*British Moralists*, paras. 563, 562).

Human Nature. Such a treatise will inform us about some matters of fact, for:

[We should] reject every system of ethics . . . which is not founded on fact and observation. . . . The hypothesis which we embrace is plain. It maintains, that morality is determined by sentiment. It defines virtue to be *whatever mental action or quality gives to a spectator the pleasing sentiment of approbation;* and vice the contrary. We then proceed to examine a plain matter of fact, to wit, what actions have this influence. . . .[3]

Later writers, like John Mackie, may find the matters of fact not quite so 'plain'. In particular, they will wish to explain why moral statements, which are neither intended by their makers nor taken by their hearers to be *about* sentiments or what influences our sentiments, are none the less *intended and taken* (a) to be capable of being simply true or false and (b) to be action-guiding *intrinsically*, i.e. not merely contingently upon their hearer's having certain sentiments, feelings, desires or inclinations. The explanation, foreshadowed by Hume, will then be in terms of some sort of 'objectification', i.e. of projection of our sentiments onto the actions (etc.) which are the objects of those sentiments, so that the evaluative and/or moral qualities

ascribed are illusory features, and the illusion is generated in a complicated way by the interplay of our sentiments in social situations in which the illusion, once established and regularly employed in interpersonal communications and shared opinions, can play an important and perhaps a useful part.[4]

Others will wish to abstain from 'inventing right and wrong'[5] on the basis of what is 'socially useful'. They will instead be content to do 'meta-ethics', considered as an analysis of the language and logic employed in the moral discourse. Instead of postulating a process of objectification to explain why people suppose that moral judgments are true (or false), they may assert (against Mackie, but in agreement with some of Hume's reductive strategies) that moral statements are not

---

[3] Hume, op. cit., secs. I and II (*British Moralists*, paras. 563, 600).

[4] Mackie, op. cit., p. 144; on 'objectification' and 'projection', ibid., pp. 72-3, 74.

[5] The phrase is the sub-title of Mackie's book *Ethics* (Penguin, Harmondsworth: 1977).

meant to be true or false. Rather, moral statements express the speaker's sentiments; or, alternatively, they prescribe, i.e. endorse a universalizable prescription or command that such-and-such an action should be done by anyone, including the speaker, in circumstances like those in question.

When I was an undergraduate, the favoured reduction of ethics was the meta-ethical theory last mentioned: ethical statements are prescriptions (quasi-imperatives), which can be of any content (no truth is at stake) provided only that the prescriber be willing to do the prescribed action himself in like circumstances. This was offered as an accurate account, not so much of human nature (which was not considered to be, as such, a topic for philosophers), but of 'our' language, 'the language of morals'.

But as an account of our language, it quickly broke down. Philosophers such as Philippa Foot soon showed that ethical prescriptions (and praise or blame or other ascriptions of rightness or wrongness or . . .) are intrinsically (i.e., she said, by the rules of our language) related to concepts of harm, advantage, benefit, importance . . . Thus 'a man cannot make his own personal decision about the considerations which are to count as evidence in morals',[6] any more than he can make his own personal decision that X (which gives offence to others) is not rude, or that Y (which injures delicate fabrics but nothing else) is to be labelled 'dangerous',[7] or that hand-clasping three times an hour is a virtue while courage is not.

But it was premature to suppose that Philippa Foot's successful argument made a clean break from the scepticism of Hobbes and Hume. That scepticism was and is a doubt not about the links between moral judgment, moral language and human nature, but about the role of *reason (considered as a an ability to discover truth)* in the formation of moral language and judgment and thus in guiding action. And Philippa Foot was soon found to be *denying* that it is *irrational* simply to reject morality.[8] 'The reasons men have for acting justly and charitably depend on contingent human

[6] Philippa Foot, 'Moral Arguments' (1958) 67 *Mind*; reprinted in Foot, *Virtues and Vices* (Basil Blackwell, Oxford: 1978), at p. 106.
[7] Foot, 'Moral Beliefs' (1958-59) 59 *Proc. Aristotelian Soc.*; reprinted in *Virtues and Vices*, at p. 116.
[8] Foot, 'Morality as a System of Hypothetical Imperatives' (1972) 81 *Phil. Rev*; reprinted in *Virtues and Vices*, at pp. 161-2.

attitudes . . .'[9] It is not the case, she said, 'that each man, whatever his desires and whatever his situation, necessarily has reason to be just'.[10] Moreover,

there is no such thing as an objectively good *state of affairs*. Such constructions as 'a good state of affairs', 'a good thing that *p*', are used subjectively, to mark what fits in with the aims and interests of a particular individual or group.[11]

I shall return later (III.3) to this contrast between 'objective' and 'subjective'. For the moment, I shall simply say that subsequent discussion has undermined Philippa Foot's thesis that moral reasons are reasons only for someone who happens to have a desire or desires of a certain sort.

As John McDowell puts it, after a careful analysis of the role of desires in reasons for action,

a failure to see reason to act virtuously stems, not from the lack of a desire on which the rational influence of moral requirements is conditional, but from the lack of a distinctive way of seeing situations. If that perceptual capacity is possessed and exercised, it yields non-hypothetical reasons for acting.[12]

McDowell, like Thomas Nagel, David Wiggins and many others, is consciously repudiating the Hobbesian and Humean claim that practical reason is founded on pre-rational desires of which all we can say is 'we happen to have them'. He is consciously aiming his account against that kind of reduction of ethics to 'human nature'.

Even so, McDowell falters in his account of the power of reason. The passage just quoted, concerning the 'perceptual capacity' to see situations morally, continues by agreeing with Foot:

Now the lack of a perceptual capacity, or failure to exercise it, need show no irrationality.

And McDowell accepts her claim that such lack of perception

---

[9] Foot (ed.), *Theories of Ethics* (OUP, Oxford: 1967), p. 9; repeated as a note added to 'Moral Beliefs' in *Virtues and Vices*, at p. 130.

[10] *Virtues and Vices*, at p. xiv.

[11] Foot, 'Reasons for Action and Desires' (1972) *Aris. Soc. Supp. Vol.* XLVI; reprinted in *Virtues and Vices*, at p. 154.

[12] McDowell, 'Are Moral Requirements Hypothetical Imperatives?', (1978) *Aris. Soc. Supp. Vol.* LII, at p. 23.

as is involved in failing to see reason to act virtuously does not amount to irrationality. Neither he nor she considers whether 'irrational' has stronger and weaker senses. They do not raise the question whether failing to see reason to act virtuously is simply *unreasonable*.

So in this chapter, I try some sorting out of the relation between desire and understanding, to help show how ethics can claim objectivity, i.e. truth. A study of the relations between desire and understanding is, in itself, a theoretical (non-practical) pursuit; and ethics is as much practical as theoretical (I.1). But the theoretical study is necessary because false theories about human capacities can undermine one's practical grasp of human good. If I come to believe that my opinions about what is good for human beings are simply a projection or objectification of desires which I happen to have (and which could conceivably be altered by technology), a whole range of genuine goods will begin to seem to me unintelligible, not worth pursuing, no good . . . This is one aspect of the complex interdependence of theoretical and practical, of anthropology and ethics.

II.2   *Desire and understanding*

Even where something is done without being reasoned out in advance, reasons for it can normally be reconstructed. Reflection on the logic of practical reasoning can therefore help us to understand practical reasonableness.

But explorations of that logic are themselves strongly dependent on an understanding of practical understanding. Take, for example, Anthony Kenny's account: the inference rules of practical reasoning ensure that one never passes from a satisfactory to an unsatisfactory proposal or plan or fiat. And, he says:

a plan is satisfactory relative to a certain set of wants, if and only if whenever the plan is satisfied every member of that set of wishes is satisfied.[13]

Thus, according to Kenny, practical reasoning aims at 'the satisfaction of the reasoner's wants'.[14]

---

[13] Kenny, *Will, Freedom and Power* (Basil Blackwell, Oxford: 1975), p. 81 (in the chapter entitled 'Practical Reasoning and Rational Appetite').
[14] Ibid., p. 89.

Caution! These terms, 'wants' and 'satisfaction' can carry you all unawares across the gulf between, say, Aristotelian and, say, Humean ethics—or between ethics and the negation of ethical responsibility. Take 'wants': I can use the phrase, 'my wants', to refer either (i) to my objectives, i.e. the things I want to get, to do, to have or to be (and these are all 'at a distance' from me here and now);[15] or (ii) to my present desires conceived of as states of my present being, my will, psyche or experience . . . to which present states correspond those future states of my being, psyche or experience which we call 'satisfaction(s)'. And that term 'satisfaction', like its cognate 'satisfying', differs widely in its connotations from the term 'satisfactory'. For the satisfactory is not, essentially, what is satisfying or creates satisfactions; rather it is what is suitable for a purpose (or even, simply, suitable, i.e. good). And the purposes we intelligently conceive and pursue via practical reasoning cannot be assumed to be exclusively, or even primarily, concerned with getting us satisfactions.

Thus, despite apparent verbal similarity, there is a radical distinction between Kenny's claim that the starting point of practical reasoning is the reasoner's *wants*, and the claim made by Anscombe (following Aristotle) that the starting point is *something wanted*.[16]

Gradually it becomes clear that Kenny's interpretation of the logic of satisfactoriness assimilates practical reasoning to a device for securing satisfactions (and in that sense satisfying 'wants'). So we find him saying that for Aristotle and Aquinas, practical reasoning concerns 'not . . . satisfactoriness, but rather goodness'. Aristotle and Aquinas, I think, would have regarded the contrast between satisfactoriness and goodness as spurious. But they would have been glad that Kenny distinguishes between satisfactoriness (and thus practical reasoning) *as he interprets it*, and the objects (goods) satisfactorily secured through practical reasoning as they interpret it. As we shall see (II.4), some who think they are expounding a theory of goods in the spirit of Aristotle and Aquinas in fact quite fail to see these important distinctions.

[15] Cf. G. E. M. Anscombe, *Intention* (Basil Blackwell, Oxford: 1958), p. viii.
[16] Anscombe, op. cit., p. vii: 'The starting point for a piece of practical reasoning is something wanted, and the first premise mentions something wanted'; also p. 62.

The upshot of Kenny's interpretation of practical reasoning is this: wants themselves are not an 'output of reason'.[17] This is tantamount to saying that at the level of basic first premises, no question of intelligibility or reasonableness can arise. Conclusions can be questioned for their satisfactoriness, and thus there can be questioning and critique of the many desires which are for things wanted as apparently satisfactory. But there will (on this view) be some desires which are beyond such questioning, which simply exist as 'natural facts' about me or about everyone, and which make practical reasoning and reasonableness possible *without themselves being matters of reason or understanding at all*.

Here we obviously have rejoined Hobbes and Hume. But not just Hobbes and Hume. A whole school of interpreters of Aristotle has claimed that when Aristotle said 'deliberation is of means not ends' he meant to ally himself with those who maintain that the basic ends of our action are provided not by our intelligent grasp of certain objectives as truly good, but rather by the desires with which human nature equips us, or which we simply happen to have. And that school of interpreters has found supporters among the many neo-scholastics who thought they were following Aquinas when they said that *prudentia* concerns means not ends, and that *synderesis* (the other aspect of reason mentioned by Aquinas in this connection) is a matter not of understanding ends but of intuiting moral truths about the fitting or the obligatory, i.e. about certain *conditions on* the pursuit of ends (the ends of human action being then supposed to be given by subrational 'inclinations'). To all these, we can add the line that runs from phenomenologists such as Brentano and Scheler through to the late works of Bernard Lonergan, in which we are said to 'apprehend' value 'in feelings', so that 'apprehension of values and disvalues is the task not of understanding but of intentional response' i.e. of 'sensibility' and 'feelings', 'feelings [which] reveal their objects'.[18]

[17] Kenny, op. cit., p. 98: 'the conclusion of a piece of practical reasoning is a description of an action to be done: a fiat concerning the reasoner's action. As a fiat it is an expression of the reasoner's wants; as the conclusion of a piece of practical inference it is the output of his reason . . .'

[18] Lonergan, *Method in Theology* (London and New York: 1972), pp. 37, 245; also pp. 67, 115. See also Lonergan, 'Natural Right and Historical Mindedness' (1977) 51 *Proc. Am. Cath. Phil. Ass.* 132 at p. 135 ('Feelings reveal values

But all this talk of wants to be satisfied, of desires and of feelings, quite misses (or at best mislocates) what is important about human action. Consider your action in attending this lecture. You are coming into this theatre and sitting down. Someone asks what you are doing; so far as an outside observer is concerned, you have perhaps been wandering around looking for somewhere to go to sleep for the night, and this looks a good spot . . .; or perhaps you are testing seats for comfort, or perhaps you've come to see friends, or to hear a lecture. The question 'What are you doing?' can be translated 'Why are you moving thus and thus?' or 'Why are you here now?', etc., i.e. a question of the form 'What for?'

Now suppose your answer was 'To hear this lecture'; further explanations could reasonably be requested. 'What for?' And the answers could be various. (i) 'I just like listening to Anglo-Australian accents'; (ii) 'I've detested this man for years, and now I've got a question that will really show him up in question-time'; (iii) 'I'm gathering material for an exposé of creeping neo-Aristotelianism in philosophy'; (iv) 'I'm interested in ethics, and I don't think I've got all the answers yet; perhaps the lecture will be some help'. And so on.

The first two of these answers make reference to feelings (of pleasure in listening, of hate, of triumph over the hated); but even here there is no claim to be feeling or experiencing anything at the time of the action of coming into the theatre; indeed we need not suppose that there is even a claim that the action is being done for the sake of getting feelings of satisfaction or of 'release' of the other feelings mentioned. Rather, those answers refer more directly to a *conception that it would be good to* have certain feelings or to satisfy certain desires which usually are appreciably *felt*; and in each case neither the entertaining of this conception nor the deciding to act and acting upon it need be accompanied (let alone constituted) by any state of feeling.

When we consider the third and fourth answers, feelings (and desires and 'satisfactions') are even more plainly not what must be mentioned in order to explain the action in question. Idiomatically, of course, we may say things like: 'I

to us'), and p. 141 ('On affectivity rests the apprehension of values').

felt that I don't know enough . . .' But the 'I felt . . .' can and should be taken as 'I realized that . . .' or 'I came to understand that . . .' And neither framing nor pursuing the idea of exposing the errors of neo-Aristotelianism (or the idea of finding out the truth about ethics) are anything like having a feeling, or an emotion, or a 'desire' in the sense of felt urge. Your wanting to find out the truth, or to expose error, consists in your thinking it would be good to find out . . ., or expose . . . It consists in your seeing the opportunity, and in seeing no reason not to take that opportunity, and in your taking the necessary steps to come. If you have feelings of anticipation or enthusiasm, they are another matter. They may be useful (though it's not that we have them *for the sake of* anything!) if there are obstacles to be overcome (tiredness, traffic jams . . .); they may, on the other hand, be deceptive or delusive and merely the prelude to feelings of frustration or desolation with the way things work out.

I am not questioning the existence or the psychological importance of feelings, emotions, inclinations, desires *qua* felt wants, etc. Rather, I am saying, *first*, that in cases like those under consideration (which are the stuff of daily life), the feelings and emotions and inclinations and 'desires' cannot even be identified without reference to the relevant *conceptions* (i) of certain things as practical possibilities, and (ii) of those possibilities as 'opportunities', i.e. as possibilities of attaining some form of good. And, *secondly*, I am saying that it is those conceptions that provide your reason for acting; it is not merely that they guide you; they also motivate you. Indeed, *seeing the point of* coming to the lecture enables you to act notwithstanding feelings which, *qua* feelings, predominantly stand in the way of coming (lassitude, irritation with the advertising, anxiety about the children at home . . .). And in that proposition, as elsewhere in my discussion, 'seeing' is just idiomatic for 'understanding'.

In short, in this standard sort of case, the question 'What are you doing?' is the question 'Why are you . . .?', and that question is relevantly answered not simply by pointing to some state of my feelings, emotions or 'desires', but primarily by referring to the action under a description that makes it intelligible as an opportunity, i.e. as having a point, i.e. as a good (not necessarily 'moral'!), i.e. as a good thing to be doing . . . now.

The term 'practical reasoning' signifies all the thinking you need, to be doing what you are doing. Reason is practical, not by merely devising intelligent ways of pursuing desires which are simply presented to one's reason as, so to say, independent of and prior to the workings of one's intelligence. Rather, reason is practical first of all by *identifying the desirable* (with a view, of course, to pursuing it thereafter and pursuing it intelligently). The desirable figures in my practical thinking not as whatever I happen to have a feeling for, or an 'independent desire' for. Rather it is that which, *qua* possible action or object of action, appears to me in a favourable light, i.e. as having a point, i.e. as somehow good to be getting, doing, having, being... This conception of something as desirable provides, typically, sufficient motivation to act.

Confusion arises in these matters from many sources. One potent source is this. Anyone who is acting voluntarily is *motivated* (as we have seen, by his reason for acting, his conception of a good to be attained by acting). The fact that he is motivated entails that we can say of him that he *wants* to be doing this act (even in those cases where he also wants not to be doing this act!). Indeed, we can say of him that he *has a desire to* be acting thus (even in those cases where he has competing desires of some sort). Then people leap to the conclusion that we have here the sort of pre-rational desire that (some) philosophers imagine provides the basis for practical reasoning. But what we really have here are desires that (if we retain the 'basis' metaphor) are based upon practical understanding. These desires can be predicated of the person involved only because he is acting or intending to act, i.e. only because he is doing something (or intending to do it) for some reason which can be fully specified without referring to a desire.

Thus we should prefer Anscombe's formulation to Kenny's. That is, we should say not that practical reasoning begins with *wants* (or desires) and seeks satisfactory ways of *satisfying* them; but that practical reasoning begins by identifying *something wanted* (or desired), i.e. something considered (*practically* considered) desirable. These things wanted are the *objects* I spoke of above (I.6). And practical reasoning goes on to seek satisfactory ways of getting, realizing or otherwise participating in this 'object', this thing wanted.

Now not everything can be intelligibly wanted. For not everything can be intelligently regarded as desirable. The mark of the desirable is that reference to it provides a non-baffling answer to the question 'What for?'. If a member of the audience at this lecture is asked 'What are you here for?' and he replies 'I want to breathe so-and-so many cubic inches of carbon dioxide into the atmosphere of this room', his reply is baffling, unintelligible as a reason for action, unless he goes on to indicate what he wants *that* for: e.g. as part of a scientific experiment or sociological observation, or as a new religious observance of a Californian type . . . If, on the other hand, he says he has come in the hope of improving his knowledge of ethics, or of current Anglo-Saxon philosophy, no further questions arise. His action, his reason for it, and his desire for it, are now quite intelligible. (Had his answer referred to his desires, that would have added nothing save emphasis to his answer). Implicitly or explicitly, his answer displays his action as a participation in, a way of realizing, one of the generic ends of human beings, one of the basic forms of human good: in this instance, the good of truth and knowledge of it.

But what if his answer were that he came to see the hated lecturer discomfited by ruthless questioning? Would that, too, count as specifying an intelligible reason for action in terms of basic human good, a generic form of human well-being? Not at all. To the extent that the desire is to see the truth that the lecturer is falsifying vindicated against the lecturer's sophistry, obstinacy, etc., the basic good at stake is the good of truth and knowledge of it. And the same good is at stake to the extent that the desire is to see a falsely inflated reputation deflated. But to the extent that the desire is to see another person damaged, in his personal comfort and/or his merited reputation, the only apparently intelligible good at stake is the experience of satisfaction that may be obtained in the moment of triumph. As the literary exploration of hatred has so often shown, that experience is dust and ashes. Hatred leads not to human goods but to their destruction, for the sake of a *simulation* of the satisfaction that comes from putting genuine goods and genuine deficiencies (say, truth and error) in their proper places. This will be confirmed, very shortly, by a thought-experiment with an 'experience machine'.

The account I have been giving, of the relation between desire and understanding in human action, is an account elaborated with much subtlety by not a few contemporary philosophers. And the stimulus to many of these accounts has been an Aristotle who is no longer read as restricting the role of reason to deliberating about means, an Aristotle no longer read as teaching that human ends are established independently of intelligence by 'desires'.

II.3   The experience machine, the critique of feelings, and human flourishing

We can better understand the relation between desire and practical understanding if we do the thought-experiment known in contemporary philosophical jargon as 'the experience machine'. This will also help us to say what it is to participate in real human goods, i.e. what is truly worthwhile.

Suppose you could be plugged into an 'experience machine' which, by stimulating your brain while you lay floating in a tank, would afford you all the experiences you choose, with all the variety (if any) you could want: but you must plug in for a lifetime or not at all. Would one choose to plug in for the sake of a lifetime of (nothing but) 'pleasures' as imagined in the early utilitarian tradition, i.e. of thrills or pleasurable tingles or other internal feelings? When we realize that we would not plug in for the sake of that sort of experience, we realise that 'pleasure' is not the point of human existence; the life of pleasure cannot really count as a life of fulfilment.

But now suppose that we consider the option of plugging in for the sake of a lifetime of *experiences of* any or all of the sorts of things (activities, achievements . . .) in which a human being can 'take pleasure' in the broadest sense of pleasure. What is on offer is a life of satisfactions, in a broad sense of 'satisfaction'. But remember, it is not a life of activities, achievements, fulfilments; it is a lifetime of doing nothing at all, but of just floating in a tank plugged into a machine which creates for you the experience of satisfactions. Such a lifetime is not to be chosen, is it?

In agreeing with me that to plug into such a lifetime would be a grievously regrettable choice (though not regretted by the one who chose so to submerge himself!), you are agreeing that how our lives feel 'from the inside' is not the only thing that matters to us. Feelings, however refined and complex, are neither the basic constituents of, nor the critical guide to, the basic forms of human good. Aristotle had this in mind when he said

no-one would choose to live with the intellect of a child throughout his life, *however much he were to be pleased at the things that please children.*[19]

Being pleasing, satisfying and, in those ways, desirable is intrinsic to something's being a human good, worthwhile, choice-worthy; but more fundamental to that worth is that the object(ive) in question be *fulfilling*, an aspect of human *flourishing*.

Robert Nozick's exploration of his thought-experiment's further implications is profound and helpful. Whether he intended it or not, his reflections resume three great themes of the Platonic and Aristotelian ethics.

A. *Activity has its own point*

Firstly, then, our rejection of the experience machine illustrates our practical understanding that good is to be found in activity. Even when the activity is constituted by contemplation, attentiveness, waiting . . . it is still radically distinguishable from the pure passivity of an experience stripped of the activity which in life outside the experience machine is both the cause and, so to speak, the content of the experience. The experience machine could give you the experience of writing a great novel or of overcoming danger in company with a friend; but in fact you would have done nothing, achieved nothing. When, in the end, your brain rotted in the tank, it could be said of you that from the time you plugged in until you died 'you never lived'.

Aristotle gives heavy emphasis to the fact that the life of *eudaimonia* is a lifetime of activity (contemplative or otherwise). The twentieth-century German Jesuits who formulated the principle of subsidiarity—that principle of justice which insists that people should not be absorbed into giant enterprises in which they are mere cogs without opportunity to

---

[19] *Nic. Eth.* X, 3: 1174a1-3.

act on their own initiative—found their inspiration in the neo-Aristotelian tag *omne ens perficitur in actu*: flourishing is to be found in *action*.

Above all, in reflecting on our reasons for not plugging in, we can begin to understand that very profound principle of Aristotle's: the decisive point of human activity (even when the activity is for the sake of producing something else) is *the activity itself*.

B. *Maintenance of one's identity is a good*

Secondly, the thought-experiment provides a context which illuminates another of Aristotle's 'no-one would . . .' principles (see I.5 above). Indeed, this is one of the most profound of them:

No-one chooses to possess the whole world if he has first to become someone else . . .[20]

It will be helpful here to juxtapose two quotations. The first is from a commentary (written before Nozick's book) on the passage from Aristotle just quoted:

To choose not to be a man is to choose not to be the one man one was, and therefore to choose death. Such a choice is obviously possible, but . . . if the good life for man is anything but a figment it plainly does not consist in suicide.[21]

The other is a fragment of Nozick's discussion of the experience machine:

A second reason for not plugging in is that we want to *be* a certain way, to be a certain sort of person. . . . There is no answer to the question of what a person is like who has long been in the tank. Is he courageous, kind, intelligent, witty, loving? It's not merely that it's difficult to tell; there's no way he is. Plugging into the machine is a kind of suicide.[22]

Each of the passages I have quoted is helpful. Neither gets to the bottom of the matter. Certainly I cannot get to the bottom of it, either. We are here confronting one of the points

[20] *Nic. Eth.* IX, 4: 1166a 19-22.
[21] Stephen R. L. Clark, *Aristotle's Man: Speculations upon Aristotelian Anthropology* (Clarendon Press, Oxford: 1975), p. 19.
[22] Robert Nozick, *Anarchy, State, and Utopia* (Basil Blackwell, Oxford: 1968), p. 43.

at which the metaphysical category 'nature' is inadequate to the reality which is grasped by ethics. (It is not the only point: the dimension of one's masculinity or femininity creates serious difficulties for the category 'human nature'. We should not be too surprised by these difficulties; epistemologically, metaphysics is the last and most difficult, not the first and most *a priori*, of the achievements of reflective understanding.) At any event, there is this good that consists not merely in my being a human being of a certain sort but in my being and continuing to be who I am. The goods that are (so far as possible) thrown away in suicide include that good. It is closely related to, but analytically distinguishable from, the good which Nozick rightly points out is thrown away by plugging in to the experience machine, viz. the good of being a person *of a certain sort*, that good which Nozick has in mind when he asks 'Why should we be concerned only with how our time is filled, *but not with what we are?*'. I think Aristotle's principle is concerned not only with the good of being '*what* we are' (i.e. of being what we, as beings with a certain nature, can be), but also with the good, for each one of us, of being *who* one is.

In reflecting on this principle, we are near bedrock. But at least two lines of thought seem to contribute to it. One is an understanding of the givenness of one's place in the cosmos, and indeed of one's self; to lose one's identity would thus be, in a sense, to lose (willingly or unwillingly) the priceless gift with which one began and which all other attainments can only supplement. The other is a line of thought I shall resume in Chapter VI: all one's free choices go to constitute oneself, so that one's own character or identity is the most fundamental of one's 'accomplishments'; the accomplishment most unequivocally one's own; and if one's character is bad there still remains the possibility of a repentance and reformation which will be as much one's own accomplishment as one's former, regrettable, accomplishments: VI.1, VI.2.

C. *Appearances are not a good substitute for reality*

I pass now to the *third* implication of an intelligent rejection of a life on the experience machine. Here we meet the master principle, perhaps, of Plato's ethics: reality is to be preferred to appearances; insight and knowledge and living-in-touch-with-reality are to be preferred to the pleasures of illusion and ignorance and living-in-a-dream. As Nozick puts it, in the experience machine 'there is no *actual* contact with any deeper reality [than that which people can construct], though the experience of it can be simulated'.[23] Opting for such a simulation would be to bury oneself in a tomb far deeper than Plato's Cave; the experience would, *ex hypothesi*, be more veridical than that of Plato's prisoners, but the actual divorce from reality would be more total than their's, since they could *actually* communicate with, for example, those who, having ascended to a clear view of reality, had returned to tell them about it.

Now notice: the distinction between being in contact with the real world of other people, etc., and having the complete but mere experience of being in contact with reality is a distinction which cannot be apprehended 'in feelings' or 'in experience'. For, *ex hypothesi*, everything that feelings and experience as such can deliver is on one side of the distinction. Yet the distinction remains; by our critical intelligence we understand both the distinction and its importance. We *understand* that the distinction between real life really lived and the self-immolating passivity of the 'indeterminate blob'[24] floating in the tank of experiences is profound and real and important.

And notice, too: when we reject or even question, in thought, the option of plugging in, we are grasping (understanding) that certain possibilities—the possibilities of activity (as distinct from the mere experience of it), of shaping and maintaining one's identity (instead of merely seeming to), and of knowing and communicating with reality and real persons (not mere semblances)—are more than bare 'factual' possibilities. We understand them instead as the sort of evaluated possibility that we call *opportunities*. That is, we understand those possible states of affairs as desirable, i.e. as important, and perhaps, in the instance under consideration, as basic, human good(s).

Thus our meditation about the experience machine can clarify and sharpen the distinction between human goods as

---

[23] Nozick, op. cit., p. 43.
[24] Id.

experienced and human goods as (not only experienced but also) intelligible. The thought-experiment unequivocally confirms that we can (and indeed typically do) opt for a good which involves bodily life and welcome experience of every sort, but which in its full measure and content as a good is discernible *only* by intelligence.

II.4   *Is understood good the good of a system for securing satisfactions?*

Everything in ethics depends on the distinction between the good as experienced and the good as intelligible. A grasp of the distinction is as important as that 'intellectual conversion' by which we overcome empiricism in general philosophy. Indeed, it is a form of that intellectual conversion, in which we come to understand how understanding grasps intelligibilities in experience and thus attains knowledge, by a process which is not like opening one's eyes or activating one's other senses. It is surprising, then, to find that the philosopher who most helpfully expounds (against empiricism) the reality and power of human understanding in the fields of science, interpretation and common sense himself misunderstands our practical understanding of human good.

Experience, questions leading to insight, reflective questions leading to rational judgment: such is the triadic schema of Bernard Lonergan's penetrating analysis of the structure of human understanding in the non-practical intellectual operations of science, interpretation and common sense. Parallel to that triad, then, he offers a triadic account of 'levels of the good'.[25] At the first level, then, is the good which is 'the object of desire', i.e. of desires and aversions which are 'prior to questions and insights, reflections and judgments'. When the good on this level is attained, it is 'experienced as pleasant, enjoyable, satisfying'. Jumping for a moment to Lonergan's third level, we find him speaking of 'good which emerges on the level of reflection and judgment, of deliberation and choice'.[26]

We can thus anticipate that this triad of levels of the good

[25] Lonergan, *Insight: a Study of Human Understanding* (London: 1957), pp. 596-7; see also p. 213, and Lonergan, *Method in Theology*, pp. 47-51.
[26] *Insight*, pp. 596-7.

is presented by Lonergan as a manifestation of the triadic structure of intellectual operations: experience, insight, judgment. And the anticipation seems justified. For the second level of the good—the crucial level, as his book's title, *Insight*, suggests—is indeed presented by him as a good which, 'while it is anticipated and reflected by spontaneous intersubjectivity, essentially is a formal intelligibility that is to be discovered only by raising questions, grasped only through accumulating insights, formulated only in conceptions', and which 'lies totally outside the field of sensitive appetition':[27] 'the intelligible good'.[28] Yes. But what are the goods thus understood?

At this decisive point, Lonergan's account seems to me to settle for a refined but unequivocal empiricism: the good as understood is 'the good of order'.[29] And the good of order is:

an intelligible pattern of relationships that condition the fulfilment of each man's desires by his contributions to the fulfilment of the desires of others and, similarly, protect each from the object of his fears in the measure he contributes to warding off the objects feared by others.[30]

Or again, the possible goods of order:

are constructions of human intelligence, possible systems for ordering the satisfaction of human desires.[31]

Certainly, Lonergan *wants* to distinguish his position from the counter-positions of 'the hedonist or sentimentalist'[32] or, generically, the empiricist. The empiricism I detect in his account of human good is refined, for (i) he points out that his 'good of order . . . cannot be identified either with desires or with their objects or with their satisfactions. For these are palpable and particular, but the good of order is intelligible and all-embracing';[33] and (ii) the desires for which satisfactions are sought include such non-sensitive desires as the desire for knowledge or virtue.[34]

Still, his position seems empiricist. For goodness seems to be located in the satisfaction of the desires that a (human)

---

[27] Id.   [28] Ibid., p. 601.   [29] Ibid., p. 597.   [30] Ibid., p. 213.
[31] Ibid., pp. 597-8; also pp. 601-2, 605; *Method in Theology*, p. 49.
[32] *Insight*, p. 606.   [33] Ibid., p. 213.
[34] Ibid., p. 596; Lonergan, *A Second Collection* (New York and London: 1974), p. 81.

being happens to have, not in the perfections attained, realized and participated in by that desiring being—the perfections which are understood first in practical reason's grasp that 'X [knowledge, life, friendship . . .] is a good to be pursued . . .' Both Hume and Aristotle correlate the term 'good' with desires and objects of desire. Lonergan seems to think that 'the good in the Aristotelian sense of the object of appetite, *id quod omnia appetunt*', corresponds to his own first level of the good.[35] But Aristotle is not only the author of that confusing tag, 'the good is what all things desire'. He is also a thoughtful adherent of an apothegm which, while it should not be taken as the last word on the relation between desire and goodness, nevertheless is as fundamental to ethics as Plato saw it was: 'we desire something because it seems good to us; it's not that it seems good to us because we desire it'.[36] For a Humean, the correlate and object of desire is *satisfaction*. For a Platonist, an Aristotelian, a Thomist, and for anyone who has accurately understood the relations between desire and understanding, the correlate and object of desire is *perfection*, i.e. what makes the one who desires *better off*, what is for him *a good thing*. Satisfaction is a good aspect of the attainment by him of that good, but it is not that good, and 'satisfying for me' is in very many cases not part of the description under which he pursues that object of desire.

In this matter, Lonergan seems on the side of Hume: 'objects of desire are instances of the good because of the satisfactions they yield', and 'the intelligible orders of human invention are a good because they systematically assure the satisfaction of desires',[37] indeed 'of all effectively desired instances of the particular good' (where 'particular good' is taken 'to include wants of every kind').[38] (We saw Kenny speaking likewise of 'satisfaction': II.2 above.)

The conclusion seems inescapable: Lonergan has overlooked the truly decisive difference between the good as merely experienced and the good as understood. Understanding and feeling are usually so integrated in our wanting that we can readily overlook or misunderstand the distinction. The

---

[35] See Lonergan, *A Second Collection*, p. 84.
[36] *Metaphysics* XII, 7: 1072a29-30.
[37] Lonergan, *Insight*, p. 605.
[38] *Method in Theology*, pp. 48, 49.

difference is this: between sheerly wanting, and wanting something (to get, to have, to do or to be) *under a description*.

We can discern this difference even in contexts where it could be easily overlooked, contexts in which a sheer, unintellectualized want seems paramount or self-sufficient: say, wanting to drink. For even here there is a real difference between, on the one hand, the experience of thirst, and on the other hand thinking that it would be nice to have a drink and therefore taking the glass and drinking from it in order to *have a drink* (rather than to see how the water tastes around here, or to make a philosophical point, or to keep my vocal chords lubricated for public speaking, or so that I won't feel thirsty later on . . .).

Once we are thus conceiving the objectives of our action, i.e. wanting and choosing them under some description, we find (as I have already said: II.2) that those descriptions either constitute or can be subsumed under yet more general conceptions, i.e. 'the conceptions of those generic (right or wrong) ends which are characteristic of human beings'[39] (though we don't usually consider these ends desirable *on the ground that* we consider them characteristic of human beings). Amongst such conceptions will be something like Lonergan's 'good of order', i.e. the good of co-operation in order to secure the realization of desires. But this good is only one amongst the goods (even the most generic goods) which are understood as we add our insight to our experience. And many of the desires to be realized (whether by co-operation or otherwise) will be for objects which are apparent only to our intelligence.

In short, the decisive shift to the level of the good-as-understood occurs well before (I'm not talking about chronology) the questions of co-operation and 'order' arise.

II.5 Desire for understood goods: 'will' and 'participation in goods'

We want things under a description. That is to say, we are intelligent and our intelligence is not merely contemplative,

---

[39] *Collected Philosophical Papers of G. E. M. Anscombe*, vol. I, p. 107.

but is also practical. This has many implications. For one thing, one can pursue an objective against the pull of all one's currently most strongly felt desires, inclinations, etc. For another thing, one can revise one's projects as one integrates one possible sort of course of action with others; for the description under which one chooses may become as broad and all-embracing as an entire 'life-plan'. For another thing, one can envisage a multiplicity of ways of getting, doing or being what one first thought of. Indeed, it becomes possible to envisage goods which are never fully attained and exhausted by any action or even a lifetime or world of lifetimes: hence the need to speak of goods which are not so much attained or realized as *participated in*.

For another thing, one can consider as desirable the participation of other people in goods of the same sort, i.e. one can think it good that other people, even people who do not engage one's affections at all, should be able to act (or to share in the results of action) under the same description: what at the level of mere feeling is radically different (his securing a good and my securing a good) becomes, at the level of understanding, significantly 'the same'. Thus it becomes possible to envisage, and commit oneself to, a co-operation which is not for the sake of 'what I can get out of it'. Someone who chooses a career in nursing envisages (typically) participation in the good of life and health; and the participation he or she has in mind is not the preservation of his or her own life or health but simply its preservation and restoration in others.

It remains important not to exaggerate the importance of co-operation and that sort of 'good of order'. Even someone who chose to plug into the experience machine would (if he was choosing at all) be acting on this second level; he would not be responding like an animal to the present tug of present and felt desire; he would be acting under the description 'pursuing and getting a lifetime of pleasure (or welcome experiences), that's the thing to do'. Such action is intelligent (even though folly), yet in no way envisages an intersubjective 'good of order'. (Although an order of co-operation is, of course, required to manufacture and maintain the experience machine, and to secure the recurrence of satisfactions, that order is not the concern of the chooser who by choosing to plug in removes himself from all possibility of co-operation.)

Will is simply the capacity to act in order to preserve or respect, realize or participate in, goods which may at the time of action be apparent only to intelligence. As we saw, such action can be regarded as the manifestation or product of a desire. But in all those many cases where the good for the sake of which we are acting is apparent only to intelligence, the desire is simply that rational appetite (*appetitus rationalis*) which, as the ancients said and Hume denied, is *in* our reason (*voluntas est in ratione*). That appetite for understood good is by no means confined to the good of co-operation, and indeed is likely to question the intelligibility, or at least the satisfactoriness, of a co-operation committed to securing (within the limits of compatibility of desires) *whatever* anyone may happen to 'effectively desire'.

The desire for goods that are recognized and appreciated only by our understanding, and are not the objects of any pre-intellectual 'desire' or 'feeling', is a desire that is not the less effective or real for being intellectual. Just such a desire may well have brought you here, against the inclinations of lassitude, irritation, etc. But having now stressed the distinction between the independently (and merely) experienced desire and the desire for understood good, I should add that the pursuit of understood good need not be either in competition with or in isolation from feelings and experiences.

Typically, success in the attainment of any goal is itself an experience, indeed an experience which is pleasurable and satisfying. What matters to us, in the last analysis, is not the emotional experience of getting knowledge, but coming to know; not the emotions of friendship, but being a friend; not the exhilarations of freedom, activity, self-direction, authenticity, etc., but consciously being free, acting, choosing with authenticity . . . But in each case, there is typically an emotional aspect to participation in one or other of these goods, and that emotion or feeling is one aspect of their reality as human goods. True, a participation in these goods which is emotionally dry and subjectively unsatisfying is still good and meaningful as far as it goes. But these goods are not participated in fully unless they are *experienced* as good. That characteristic human experience of good we call emotion or (intensional) feeling. Such full participation in good is the opportunity made possible by our bodily/intellectual nature, given favourable circumstances.

Talk about all these matters is complicated, as you will have noticed, by the fact that 'desire' can be used to denote pre-rational desires but also denotes part of what it is to be intelligent. 'Experience', too, is a term that may be used to denote that which we are aware of *before* questioning and understanding; but the term extends also to the awareness that we have in understanding and wanting goods which are anticipated only intellectually and not by or in our feelings.

If, like Plato and Aristotle, we are realistic about human existence, we will add one more point about the relation between experience (feelings, 'desires', etc.) and understanding. The point can be made by changing the conditions of the experience machine, so that it is no longer necessary to opt either for a lifetime or for no time on the machine. Then we should warn anyone contemplating a limited period on the machine that he had better arrange *in advance* for someone else to unplug him. For anyone plugged into the machine is unlikely to be capable, *de facto*, of understanding the desirability of those goods of activity, authenticity and reality which give reason for unplugging; or, if he can in some sense understand those goods while submerged in his world of mere experience, he is unlikely to be motivated by them. Both our powers of intelligent discernment and our intelligent desire to act intelligently (i.e. for the sake of understood goods) are likely to be overwhelmed by the massively possessive experience of feelings, satisfactions, etc. Some such submerging of reason by passions is well-known to us in our own daily life, is it not?

II.6   *Thin theories of human good*

A theory of the good is a thin theory if and only if it offers to identify as the basic human goods those goods which *any* human being would need *whatever his objectives*. The label 'thin theory' comes from John Rawls, and is applied by him to his own account. Notice that a thin theory of the good will also be a thin theory of practical reason: the goods identified by a thin theory will be what it is rational for any human being to want whatever else his or her preferences. Thin theories of the good abound. For Rawls, the 'primary goods' are 'liberty and opportunity, income and wealth, and above all self-respect'. What here interests me about this list is the rationale of its construction. These goods are said to be primary because 'they are in general necessary for the framing and execution of a rational plan of life', i.e. *any* rational plan of life. To the extent that Lonergan's 'good of order' is offered as *the* intelligible good (II.4 above) we have a thin theory of the good as *whatever* 'ensures the recurrence of all *effectively desired* instances of the particular good [i.e. of objects or actions that meet the wants ('of every kind') of individuals] '.[40] And, to take an example from a perhaps unexpected source, we find Peter Geach offering an account of the four cardinal virtues (practical wisdom, justice, courage and temperance) in terms of them being needed, like health and sanity, for *any* large-scale enterprise.[41] He thus follows the strategy of Hobbes, whose political philosophy he admires. But unlike Hobbes, he thinks Aristotle was right to want an answer to the question 'What are men for?', i.e. to try to determine 'the end and good of man'. Geach thinks one can get a long way without answering that question. Hobbes, on the other hand, rejects the question with scorn.[42] That rejection was the corollary of his theory that practical reason is the slave of the passions (I use Hume's phrase), and it provided the (usually) tacit presupposition of most of the modern thin theories of the good.

The motivations of thin theories range from the open scepticism of Hobbes, through the tentative and moderate scepticism of a Philippa Foot (II.1 above) to the curiously political epistemology of Rawls: one must be 'democratic' in assessing the excellences of other people—at least when constructing one's theory of justice.[43] Very commonly the

---

[40] Lonergan, *Method in Theology*, p. 49.
[41] Geach, *The Virtues*, p. 16, actually says 'any large-scale worthy enterprise', but the context makes clear that 'worthy' is here given a restricted (thin) meaning: e.g. co-operation and mutual trust are explained as needed because without them 'our lives would be nasty, brutish, and short'.
[42] Hobbes, *Leviathan*, ch. XI (Raphael, *British Moralists*, para. 44)
[43] John Rawls, *A Theory of Justice* (Cambridge, Mass.: 1971; Oxford: 1972), p. 527.

motivation is fear that anything other than a thin theory of the good will entail an authoritarian politics.

The fear is unwarranted; start the list of counter-examples with John Stuart Mill and Vatican II. Nor, in any case, is it permissible (i.e. philosophically reasonable) to allow one's reflective understanding or account of the human goods to be tailored to one's fear that human liberty and authenticity will be prejudiced, in the political life of one's community, by one's philosophical findings. After all, liberty and authenticity are goods, too. They will find their proper place in any accurate (i.e. 'full', non-emaciated . . .) theory of human good. Indeed, only such a theory can make secure for them the dignity of being recognized as objective goods, truly worthwhile (rather than merely the matrix for the pursuit of 'subjective' desires and satisfactions).

Thin theories of the good are arbitrary. For the sake (typically) of consensus, in philosophy and in society, the thin theorist closes his eyes to whole ranges of human opportunity. He either declares them to be, or treats them as if they were, matters of taste, subjective opinion, individual desire . . . rather than what they are: opportunities to participate in real goods, in really worthwhile aspects of human flourishing. Thus he severs ethical inquiry at its root. For ethics is nothing worth doing if it is not an unblinkered search for the truly worthwhile in order to participate in the truly worthwhile in all its available aspects: I.1-2. Once that objective of ethics is set aside, even the meditation about the experience machine (II.3) can miscarry into a decision to plug in: that, after all, is the option favoured by those many who place their hope in Nirvana. To allow arbitrary restrictions on the practical search for true human goods is to undermine (render inconsistent) the critique of a life spent pursuing satisfying experiences. Indeed, it is to lend colour to that Hobbesian view which underlies (perhaps is a consequence of) the Hobbesian denial of objective human goods: the view that human beings *are* machines for having experiences.

II.7   The identification of basic human goods

In Chapter IV of *Natural Law and Natural Rights*, I have argued for a list of seven basic aspects of human well-being:

life, knowledge, play, aesthetic experience, sociability (friendship), practical reasonableness and religion. There I have pointed to the empirical anthropological literature which can aid our reflective identification of those basic goods and help us to test the view that they are an exhaustive list. There too, I have argued that all are equally fundamental, that there is no single, objective hierarchy of basic human goods.

I will not repeat any of those arguments here. My concern in this lecture has been to elucidate the language we use when we speak of human 'goods' and of 'understanding' human opportunities, goods, flourishing . . . My method has been the method of practical understanding and reasoning itself. That involves attention both to one's own inclinations and to the whole range of possibilities open to one. By an insight which is not an 'intuition' (because it is not made in the absence of data, nor by any 'noticeable' intellectual act) and not a deduction or inference from one *proposition* to another, one understands some of those inclinations as inclinations towards *desirable* objects, and some of those possibilities as opportunities rather than dead-ends. Because feelings and desires and inclinations of every kind are, as I have just indicated, a part of this coming to understand human goods, the whole process is peculiarly liable to be misunderstood when we come to reflect on it philosophically. Hence the famous misdescriptions which I cited at the beginning of this chapter.

The only reliable critique of those misdescriptions is one in which one proceeds by reflecting on one's own wanting, deciding and acting; and this reflection must not be an attempt to peer inside oneself, or to catch oneself as it were in a mirror out of the corner of one's eye: those empiricist methods, based on the uncritical fancy that understanding is just a matter of opening one's eyes (or other senses) and looking, yield nothing but illusions. Reflection on practical reasoning and human action is truly empirical when it seeks to understand human capacities by understanding human acts and to understand those acts by understanding their object(ive)s. Thus the revealing question is the question 'Why?', not interpreted blankly as if one were investigating iron filings jumping to a magnet or the ricochet of billiard balls, but humanly and intelligently as 'What for?' Only thus will one be able to describe one's actions as they really are, and oneself as the agent one really is. And only thus will the relations between desire and understanding in the identification and pursuit of human goods be accurately known.

Hence my reflections on your action in coming to this lecture, and on the doing of ethics, and on the possibility of plugging into an experience machine. In the course of those reflections we identified more than one basic human good: firstly, knowledge; and secondly a complex of activity, individual authenticity or identity, and living contact with reality, a complex which I am inclined to call 'practical reasonableness'. As I have said, these are by no means the only basic aspects of human opportunity; I mentioned five other aspects of human full-being. The goods of knowledge and practical reasonableness I selected for particular attention just because they are perhaps more immediately available for our reflection; the performance of reflection is the very activity that we at present want and have chosen to engage in. Moreover, it is not so easy for Hobbesian or other empiricists to explain away these two goods as mere objects of feelings we happen to have.

But my critique of those reductive explanations is not yet complete.

We have seen (II.2) that when one pursues the question 'What for?' to the point where no further such question is intelligent, one arrives, not at a 'contingent desire' or state of feeling . . . to be explained in turn by the mechanics, biology and/or psychology of 'human nature'. Rather, one arrives at the perception (i.e. the understanding or intelligent discernment) of a basic form of human flourishing in which, not one human being on one occasion, but somehow all human beings in appropriate circumstances can participate. Now, as John McDowell said, 'the lack of a perceptual capacity, or failure to exercise it, need show no irrationality' (see II.1 above). Taking 'need' strictly, that is true. But where the perception in question is so radically an intellectual perception, and the subject-matter is so central to the role of reason in anyone's life, we are bound to say that lack of *this* perceptual capacity, or failure to exercise it, *is* irrational—just as we should say that failure in perception of elementary logical relations (e.g. *modus ponens*), or of simple induction (e.g.

of causes and effects in human actions), was a manifestation of irrationality.

Still, we cannot leave our reflections on objectivity at this point. For one thing, the person whom Philippa Foot and John McDowell deny is irrational is a person who sees no reason to act *virtuously*. And thus far I have said nothing about virtue, nothing about good in the strictly moral sense. On the contrary, I have been talking about that understanding of human goods which *creates the moral problem*. Here are all these real goods, these real opportunities of flourishing, for myself and other human beings. What then am I to do? How are my choices to be reasonable, within the vast field of opportunity which an understanding of these goods makes evident? Identification of these basic goods may make clear what choices would be simply irrational in a strong sense of 'irrational'. But what are the principles, if any, which determine that choices, though not in that strict sense 'irrational', are still unreasonable, i.e. wrong? And: we have been talking throughout about goods (and implicitly, therefore about 'bads' or, say, harms); but what about right and wrong? How do those terms, understood 'morally', make practical sense?

So my response to the sceptical denial of objectivity in ethics cannot appropriately be concluded except in the context of a consideration of what I shall call the *requirements of practical reasonableness*.

NOTES

II.1

Philippa Foot's scepticism about practical reason . . . For a diagnosis antedating her later and clearer professions of this scepticism, see Finnis, 'Reason, Authority and Friendship in Law and Morals', in Khanbai, Katz and Pineau (eds.), *Jowett Papers 1968-1969* (Basil Blackwell, Oxford: 1970), esp. pp. 112-23.

II.2

The starting point for practical reasonings is something wanted . . . i.e. *to orekton*: Aristotle, *de Anima* III, 10: 433a17-21; Aquinas, *in III de Anima*, nos. 821-6.

Brentano and Scheler: 'cognition of values by feelings' . . . On Brentano (and on the whole topic of the relation between feeling, emotion and understanding), see Anscombe, 'Will and Emotion', in *Collected Philosophical Papers of G. E. M. Anscombe*, vol. I, pp. 100-7. On Max Scheler, see Karol Wojtyla, *The Acting Person* (Reidel, Dordrecht, Boston and London: 1979), pp. 248, 315 n. 71.

II.3

Human activity's decisive point is the activity itself . . . See *Nic. Eth.* VI, 4: 1140b4-6; II, 4: 1105a31-2; John M. Cooper, *Reason and Human Good in Aristotle* (Harvard UP, Cambridge, Mass.: 1975), pp. 2, 78, 111.

II.4

Lonergan on the 'good of order' . . . In Lonergan's later work, there are clear signs that what he calls the good of order is not intended by him to occupy the whole of the space which I would call the realm of basic understood goods. As I have pointed out (II.2, p. 32, footnote 18), he denies that goods ('values') are understood, and affirms that their 'apprehension is the task *not of understanding* but of intentional response [a response which is] all the fuller, all the more discriminating, the better a man one is, the more refined one's *sensibility*, the more delicate one's *feelings*': *Method in Theology*, p. 245, emphases added. Thus he speaks of 'apprehensions of value [occurring] in social, cultural, personal and religious values', 'the ontic value of persons', and 'the qualitative value of beauty, understanding, truth, virtuous acts, noble deeds'; and in *Method in Theology* the 'good of order' appears as a social value 'which conditions the vital values of the whole community' and which, while outranking the 'vital values' of health, strength, etc., is itself outranked by 'cultural' and 'personal' values: pp. 31-2, 38, 54. It remains unclear how all this is to be reconciled with the triadic structure implicitly used in the analysis in *Insight* of levels of the good; and equally unclear how the 'values' are to be related to the dichotomy between particular good and good of order (pp. 48-50). Further confusion is caused by the slogan (p. 27) 'What is good, always is concrete', which generates tangles such as the following (p. 49):

> my education was for me a particular good. But *education for everyone that wants it is another part of the good of order . . .* It is to be insisted that the good of order is . . . quite concrete. It is the actually functioning *or malfunctioning* set of 'if—then' relationships guiding operators and coordinating operations. (Emphasis added.)

Lonergan speaks of 'judgments of value' which distinguish between true and apparent goods, but the ultimate criterion of such truth seems to be yet another 'feeling': the feeling of 'a peaceful or uneasy conscience' (p. 40; also pp. 41, 35).

'The good is what all things desire' v. *the good is what makes better-off . . .* See Finnis, *NLNR*, pp. 78-9.

II.5

Will, intelligence and acting under a description . . . See Anscombe, *Collected Papers*, vol. I, pp. 105, 107, 75-7; *Intention*, secs. 36-40.

Will and reason: 'Voluntas est in ratione' . . . Aristotle, *de Anima*, III, 9: 432b5-7; for other references and brief discussion see Finnis, *NLNR*, p. 338 n. 37.

II.6

Full (non-thin) theories of the good do not entail authoritarian politics . . . See J. S. Mill, *On Liberty* (1859); Second Vatican Council, Declaration on Religious Liberty (*Dignitatis Humanae*) (1965), esp. paras. 2, 3, 7, 9, 11, 14; and Pastoral Constitution on the Church in the Modern World (*Gaudium et Spes*) (1965), esp. paras. 14-16, 39, 51, 79, 80, 89.

Hobbes's conception of human beings as machines for having experiences . . . See Hobbes, *Human Nature: or the Fundamental Elements of Policy* (1650), ch. VII (*British Moralists*, paras. 3-4); *Leviathan* (1651), ch. VI (*British Moralists*, paras 23-6). For Hobbes's denial of objective goods, see ibid., para. 25; for his denial of a highest good, see paras. 4 and 44; for his denial of the Aristotelian methodology of understanding powers and acts through understanding their objects, see para. 22.

III
Objectivity, Truth and Moral Principles

III.1 Scepticism and objectivity

The sceptic who contends that ethics is subjective—that moral principles are objectively neither true nor false but merely matters of taste and convention—has a healthy and justified concern: that we should not live deluded. He is concerned to remove (at least for himself) the illusion of objectivity created by moral language with its talk of the right and the wrong, the truly good and the really bad. His concern is for the comfortless truth that is, he thinks, masked by these conventional forms and formulae.

The sceptic's concern is in fact a form of the very concern that can stimulate us to identify true moral principles. Even if he does not care whether other people live in illusion or enlightenment, the sceptic wants to be reasonable, himself, in his beliefs about the world and human conduct. And that concern to be reasonable is what should lead us from an understanding of human opportunities to a set of choices amongst those opportunities, choices which are not merely intelligent but also reasonable. And what we call correct moral principles are simply an expression of the requirements of reasonableness in choosing ways of living. To put it another way, moral virtues are the attitudes, habits, dispositions, willingnesses . . . which can be justified as reasonable modes of response to the opportunities which intelligence makes evident to us. (On the moral language of virtues, see VI.1.)

So in this chapter I shall be exploring simultaneously both (i) the objectivity (of moral propositions) which the sceptic seeks to put in doubt and (ii) the objectivity (of moral agents) which the sceptic values and which seems to him to require his sceptical denials (but which to others seems to require and generate ethics and moral life). Reasonableness, I shall argue, requires us to reject radical scepticism as both unjustified and literally self-refuting, and also to acknowledge a whole set of requirements which make sense of moral rules and virtues.

The sceptic's two main arguments are what John Mackie called the argument from queerness and the argument from relativity (i.e. from the variety of differing moral opinions).

III.2   *The argument from queerness*

If there were objective values, then they would be entities or qualities or relations of a very strange sort, utterly different from anything else in the universe. Correspondingly, if we were aware of them, it would have to be by some special faculty of moral perception or intuition, utterly different from our ordinary ways of knowing everything else.[1]

Or again, John Mackie asked: when we say that an act is wrong because it is a piece of deliberate and gratuitous cruelty, we mean to refer to a supposedly objective moral quality (wrongness) which is somehow consequential on the natural facts about the act (its hurtfulness, its deliberateness, its gratuitousness, etc.);

But just what *in the world* is signified by this 'because'? . . . [some faculty] must be postulated which can see at once the natural features that constitute the cruelty, and the wrongness, and the mysterious consequential link between the two. Alternatively, the intuition required might be the perception that wrongness is a higher order property belonging to certain natural properties; but what is this belonging of properties to other properties, and how can we discern it? How much simpler and more comprehensible the situation would be if we could replace the moral quality with some sort of subjective response which could be causally related to the detection of the natural features on which the supposed quality is said to be consequential.[2]

In these thoughts, which make progress in many minds, we can detect the echo of David Hume's famous rhetoric:

can there be any difficulty in proving, that vice and virtue are not matters of fact, whose existence we can infer by reason? Take any action allowed to be vicious: wilful murder, for instance. Examine it in all lights, and see if you can find that matter of fact, or real existence, which you call *vice*. In whichever way you take it, you find only certain passions, motives, volitions, thoughts [i.e. of the murderer]. There is no other fact in the case. The vice entirely escapes you, so long as you consider the object. You can never find it, till you turn your reflection into

---

[1] J. L. Mackie, *Ethics: Inventing Right and Wrong* (Penguin, Harmondsworth: 1977), p. 38.   [2] Ibid., p. 41.

your own breast, and find a sentiment of disapprobation, which arises in you, towards this action. . . . Vice and virtue, therefore, may be compared to sounds, colours, heat and cold, which, according to modern philosophy [Hume means Locke's] are not qualities in objects, but perceptions in the mind . . .[3]

How are we to respond to these challenges to the view that judgments about human good and bad, and right and wrong, can really (objectively) be true or false? We should not begin our response by postulating any doctrine of truth or objectivity. Instead we should see what conception of truth and objectivity is implicit in the statements of the sceptics, and in their performance in putting forward those statements for our acceptance.

Let us take a proposition asserted by John Mackie; any one will do, so let us take one that relates to the very topic of our present inquiry:

We get the notion of something's being objectively good, or having objective value, by reversing the [actual] direction of dependence here, by making the desire depend upon the goodness, instead of the goodness on the desire.[4]

This is Mackie's theory of objectification: supposedly objective qualities of acts, states of affairs, etc., are really just the projection of feelings and wants. Mackie thinks his theory is true; he *asserts* the proposition or propositions which I just quoted. Now my quotation was itself a collection of sounds in the air, marks on the page; those sounds or marks were intended to mean, and in fact meant, the proposition. But intentions are *utterly different* from anything else in the universe. And the relationship between expression and proposition, the relationship which we call meaning, is utterly different from anything else in the universe. And that quality of the proposition which we call its truth is (whatever our account of truth) utterly different from anything else in the universe.

If you take as your model of *entities, qualities and relations* just those entities, qualities and relations which will figure in physical, chemical, biochemical . . . theories (and if you do

---

[3] Hume, *A Treatise of Human Nature* (1740), Book III, Part I, sec. 1 ('Moral distinctions not derived from reason') (Raphael, *British Moralists*, para. 503).
[4] Mackie, *Ethics*, p. 43.

not ask any questions about what it is for something to be a theory and for a theory to be a true theory), then you will be inclined to say that intentions, meanings and truth are utterly queer, and that the understanding of intentions and meanings and the adjudging of truth or falsity are so different from observing, inspecting, surveying, measuring and comparing that one had better give that understanding and adjudging the label 'special faculty of intuition', i.e. fishy.

Still, any project of explaining away intention and the understanding of it, or meaning and the understanding of it, or truth and the assessing of it, is a manifestly arbitrary and self-refuting project. The world in which we intend, mean, and assert true and false propositions, just is unimaginably more queer, i.e. diverse in its fundamental aspects, qualities and relationships, than it appears (we must suppose) to a cat that notices a bowl of milk and drinks it.

So, when we find someone reluctant, like Mackie, to think that goodness could 'belong' to certain states of affairs, because the blank question 'What is this belonging?' gets in his way, we should ask him whether that belonging is a whit more mysterious than the 'belonging' of intentions to acts, of meaning to expressions, of truth or falsity or provability to propositions . . . Some picture or model of the belonging of 'natural' properties to 'natural' objects is getting in his way. Similarly, a naive picture of causal relationships is getting in his way when he asks (about the judgment 'that is wrong because it is cruel'): 'What *in the world* is signified by this "because"?'. We can and should reply that the relationship signified by that 'because' is no more and no less 'in the world' than that signified by the 'because' in 'He ought to affirm the conclusion of that argument *because* its premises are true and the inferences valid' or 'The conclusion must be true *because* the premises are true and the inferences valid'.

In each case, when we observe that the picture or model to which Mackie implicitly appealed cannot accommodate even the simplest facts about intention, meaning and truth—facts instantiated by every one of his own assertions—we are entitled to conclude that his talk about queerness and special faculties in relation to our judgments about the good and the bad, the right and the wrong, fails to give any reason for doubt about the objectivity or truth of such judgments.

Such judgments, remember, are of the form: 'It is (or was) good for JM (or anyone else)—it really is (or was)—for him to understand the truth about good and evil, and bad for him (or anyone else) to be in a muddle about it'. Or (remembering that it is the 'objective prescriptivity' of practical judgments that seems to Mackie most queer and objectionable) of the form: 'In thinking things through, I *ought* to attend to the evidence, and if the evidence is that such-and-such, and I see no reason to doubt it, I *ought* to adjudge or accept that such-and-such' (the 'oughts' here are both theoretical and practical). What reason is there to doubt the objectivity, or truth, of either of those practical judgments? What reason is there to seek to reduce either of them to the status of mere 'objectifications' of some 'subjective response' that we (who? the speaker? or JM?) are supposed to have to a 'stimulus' provided by the 'natural features' (what features?) of the world?

Notice that the examples I just gave of practical propositions happened to concern the good of objectivity—i.e. both the objectivity that propositions have by being true, and the objectivity that persons have by being attentive to evidence, clear-headed and willing to follow an argument to the conclusion that ought to be affirmed. As I must keep insisting, that good is not the only basic and intrinsic form of good that we can understand when we consider what to think, to do and to be. My real flourishing, or JM's, has quite a number of aspects. I focused on the good of objectivity just because that happened to be the good directly at stake in deciding whether or not all propositions about good lack the objectivity of being true.

Elsewhere, I have set out rather more elaborately an argument that scepticism about the good of truth and knowledge is self-refuting.[5] I shall not repeat that here.

III.3   *Objectivity and truth*

Those philosophers who have recently been showing up the inaccuracy of the Hobbesian/Humean account of practical reason as starting from pre-rational desires, and the inaccuracy

[5] Finnis, 'Scepticism, Self-refutation, and the Good of Truth', in Hacker and Raz (eds.), *Law, Morality, and Society: Essays in honour of H. L. A. Hart* (Clarendon Press, Oxford: 1977), pp. 247-67, at pp. 250-4, 258-66; *Natural Law and Natural Rights*, pp. 73-5.

of that reading of Aristotle which reads him as an early
Humean, have also given much attention to the notions of
objectivity and truth.

Thomas Nagel, for example, has traced in a variety of
contexts how we can strive for an objectivity which would
consist in having a conception of the world which is not the
view from anywhere in the world, and which abstracts from
the individual observer's position in the world, and from
what differentiates the observer from all other beings. But
Nagel recognizes that, in *this* sense of 'objective', 'not everything is better understood the more objectively [in this
sense] it is viewed'.[6] Failure to shift decisively from this
special sense of objectivity, and to replace it with the more
adequate heuristic notion of the objective as whatever is the
case whether or not anyone judges it to be so, leads Nagel
himself to a weird dualism, according to which his 'true self'
'views the world through the eye, the person, the daily life
of TN, as through a window'.[7]

More generally, we must say that it is scientistic, not
scientific, to impose on the quest for knowledge the restriction that knowledge is only of that which can be regarded
impersonally, externally, naturalistically. Our concern is to
come to know what is so, to attain an accurate view. The
proposed restriction extends the postulates of the methods
of the natural sciences into fields of inquiry where those
methods in fact block or obscure any accurate view. Among
those fields are those that concern experience; as the title of
one of Nagel's essays asks: What is it like to be a bat? We do
not know, since we do not share that experience and cannot
adopt the point of view of the creature that has it. Yet our
own (human) subjective experiences are not altogether
private; on the contrary, as Nagel says, they are intersub-
jectively available: we can *know* what is the quality of each
other's experiences.[8] I would add that we likewise can know
what in fact are, and what it is like to have, each other's
perceptions, beliefs, doubts, aspirations, disinclinations,
intentions, decisions, regrets. Yet all these are thoroughly

---

[6] Nagel, 'The Limits of Objectivity' in Sterling McMurrin (ed.), *The Tanner
Lectures on Human Values 1980* (University of Utah Press, Salt Lake City, and
CUP, Cambridge and London: 1980), p. 78.   [7] Ibid., p. 94.
[8] Thomas Nagel, *Mortal Questions* (CUP: 1979), pp. 172, 207, 208.

subjective, and would have no place in the world if the world were just as it is conceived 'objectively', i.e. naturalistically or scientistically. Thus, someone who seeks to limit the range of reason to what can be known with *that* sort of objectivity is himself lacking in objectivity.

You will remember Philippa Foot's unqualified assertion (see II.1 above) that

there is no such thing as an objectively good *state of affairs*. Such constructions as 'a good state of affairs', 'a good thing that *p*', are used subjectively, to mark what fits in with the aims and interests of a particular individual or group.[9]

This denial of objectivity gets its plausibility from that sense of 'objectivity' which concerns the relations of things to-each-other-and-not-to-us, particularly the relations which are the concern of the natural sciences. She was complaining about Nagel's tendency to talk of 'objective values' which would constitute reasons, not merely for anyone and everyone to act, but 'for the *occurrence* of the things of which they hold true'.[10] I think she was right to question whether one can assert both (a) 'it is good for X to occur or happen' and (b) 'the value of X's occurring is altogether independent of the interests or concerns of any person in the universe'. I return to that issue in VI.3 below. But once we have seen that there is not just one straightforward contrast to be made between 'objective' and 'subjective', we are not going to be content with her simple denial of objectivity to any and every assertion that X is a good state of affairs.

The states of affairs whose goodness is in question in ethics are, primarily, the states of human beings. Describing my condition as 'well-being' does indeed 'mark what fits in with my interests'. But we should not allow Philippa Foot to bolster her assertion of subjectivity by trading on the ambiguity of the word 'interests'. No doubt we cannot detach the meaning of 'good' and 'well-being' from the notion of 'taking an interest in'; for we cannot detach the notion of good from the notion of what it is intelligent to take an interest in (favour, promote . . .). But what is *in my interests*

---

[9] Foot, *Virtues and Vices*, p. 154.
[10] Thomas Nagel, *The Possibility of Altruism* (Clarendon Press, Oxford: 1970), p. 91; also p. 120n.

is certainly not sufficiently to be determined by asking what I *happen* to *take an interest in* (desire, aim for . . .). The decisive question always is what it is *intelligent* to take an interest in. There are no 'interests' (desires . . .) that are immune from that question. Accordingly, there is no reason to assume that the answer to that question is provided by desires (even 'standard desires')[11] or feelings, or by reference to 'the fact that some people do care about such things'.[12] So there is no reason to deny the objectivity—i.e. the intelligibility and reasonableness and *truth* . . .—of statements about what constitutes someone's well-being (and is *therefore* in his interests).

David Wiggins's investigations of *truth* converge on a very similar conclusion. Objectivity is fundamentally a matter of ratiocination towards truth.[13] And what are the marks of truth? His answer is developed by way of a recapitulation of much recent philosophical work on the relations between meaning and truth. That work has concentrated on elucidating meaning in terms of truth; Wiggins exploits it to elucidate truth in terms of meaning. I shall first summarize his recapitulation, largely in my own words.

The meaning of an individual sentence *s* is understood by someone who can provide a translation *p* which is an accurate interpretation in that *s* is true if and only if *p* is true. But *p* is itself, of course, a sentence in need of understanding and thus the provision of a satisfactory translation, in any language capable of expressing indefinitely many translatable sentences, requires an accurate understanding of (i.e. a 'descriptive anthropology' which renders intelligible) the beliefs, attitudes and intentions of speakers of that language in the environments in which they use it. Conversely, if we know that *s* is accurately translated by *p*, in the sense of 'accurate translation' just explained, we are in a position to offer an explanation of the phrase 'is true' in the theorem ('theory of truth', in Tarski's sense) '*s* is true if and only if *p* is true . . .' That explanation, as worked out by Wiggins,

<hr />

[11] Cf. Foot, *Virtues and Vices*, p. xiii.
[12] Cf. ibid., p. 170.
[13] David Wiggins, 'Truth, Invention and the Meaning of Life' (1977) 62 *Proc. British Academy* 331 at p. 343; 'Truth and Interpretation', in Haller (ed.), *Proceedings of the Fourth International Wittgenstein Symposium, Kirchberg 1979* (Reidel, Boston: 1980) 36 at p. 47.

identifies the 'marks of truth', i.e. it sets out some 'truisms about truth'. The general form of his argument for each is that a property must have this mark if it is to be that property which sentences must have (or be capable of having) if they are to be susceptible of a translation which is assessable as accurate in the way just described (interpretation and descriptive anthropology . . .). There result the following five truisms about truth.

(i) Truth is the property that declarative sentences must normally be construed as aiming to enjoy. (ii) A second mark of the truth of a sentence *s* is that under favourable conditions of investigation—and notably when the investigators are open to evidenced argument—there will be a tendency for disagreement to diminish and for *s* to command agreement amongst the investigators. (iii) Every statement that lacks truth lacks it independently of a speaker's means of recognizing it, and every statement which is true possesses truth independently both of a speaker's means of recognizing it and of his will to make the statement. These first three marks of truth condense into a fourth: (iv) Every true sentence is true in virtue of something somehow (however indirectly) accessible to both speaker and interpreter. (v) Every true sentence is compatible, i.e. co-assertible, with every other true sentence.

The value of Wiggins's elucidation of truth is that, without relativizing truth, it obviates the misunderstanding that every correspondence theory of truth is prey to: that we have some access to the 'facts' or 'reality' to which true judgments and thus true statements and sentences correspond *other than the access afforded by our truth-seeking inquiries, understanding and judgments.* The illusion which underpins most denials of the objectivity of ethics is this: that to which true judgments have their truth by corresponding ('the facts', 'the world', 'reality' . . .) somehow lies open to an inspection conducted otherwise than by rationally arriving at true judgments of the type in question (scientific, historical, cryptographic . . ., and, why not? evaluative . . .). That illusion is the root of all those reductive programmes which we call philosophical empiricism—programmes like those of Hobbes and Hume and successors of theirs such as John Mackie.

You will remember that the passage of Hume which I quoted above, arguing that virtue and vice are not matters of rational judgment and fact (because not to be found when an action is 'examined in all lights'), concludes that in this respect our statements about moral qualities are like our statements about what Locke called 'secondary qualities': they appear to be about the qualities of objects but in truth are only about 'perceptions in the mind'. This use of the term 'perception' is not entirely frank; for, in ordinary speech, perception is of objects. What Hume means is quite clear: both moral (and evaluative) and 'secondary' qualities are nothing other than feelings, i.e. states of our (the speakers') being (i.e. our subjectivity), which we project onto the real objects to which we ascribe them as 'qualities'. Wiggins's next move is to turn this sort of argument against those who deny objectivity and truth to judgments of value. The conclusion will be that knowledge is not necessarily subjective merely because it is in some respects inevitably anthropocentric.

He takes one of the Lockian secondary qualities which Hume had in mind: colour. Postboxes in England are seen as red because they *are* red; their redness is 'an external, monadic property of a postbox'. ' "Red postbox" is not short for "red to human beings postbox" '.[14] Instead, what should be said is that redness is an 'anthropocentric category':

pillar-boxes, painted as they are, count as red only because there actually exists a perceptual apparatus (e.g. our own) which discriminates, and learns on the basis of direct experience to group together, all and only the *de facto* red things.[15]

Contemporary non-cognitivists in ethics do not want to be sceptics about colour or about all the myriad categories which are what they are because human observers and thinkers and doers are as they are. But though they do not *want* to deny objectivity to everything save the 'primary qualities', that would be the upshot if their arguments against the objectivity of value properties and value judgments were valid. For those arguments turn out to be arguments against the use of 'anthropocentric' predicates. And if all such categories were to be banished from the language of rational belief (i.e. from the ambit of truth), we would be left with a conceptual scheme which would 'not even have the expressive

---

[14] Wiggins, 'Truth, Invention and the Meaning of Life', at p. 349.
[15] Ibid., pp. 348-9.

resources to pick out the extensions of "red", "chair", "earth-quake", "person", "famine" . . .'[16]

Starting out with the idea that value properties are mental projections, [modern non-cognitivists] have discovered that if value properties are mental projections then, except for the primary qualities, all properties are mental projections.

And that is a *reductio ad absurdum*, in more senses of 'reduction' than one! Wiggins's conclusion, then, is clear.

It is either false or senseless to deny that what valuational predicates stand for are properties in a world. It is neither here nor there that these value properties are not primary qualities, provided only that they be objectively discriminable and can impinge upon practical appreciation and judgement. No extant argument shows that they cannot.[17]

Judgments about what is worthwhile, good, valuable, etc. can be true, objectively true, in the rich and straightforward sense of 'truth' that he has elucidated. Many such judgments about the good can, indeed, be described as factual. There is no clear distinction between fact and value; for no clear sense can be given to 'factual' other than 'objective and true', and there are many value judgments that are objective and true.[18]

III.4   *From 'good' to 'right': from value judgment to choice*

Just at this point, Wiggins falters. And just at this point, Aquinas's ethical theory leaves an unfilled gap, a gap which others have proposed to fill with rival pretenders to the imagined role of 'the master principle of ethics'.

The point I have just reached, by following through Wiggins's argument about the objectivity of evaluations, is also the point at which I ended Chapter II: there are many basic forms of human good, all equally or incommensurably basic and none reducible to any or all of the others; none of these is attainable by any one choice or finite set of choices; to commit oneself to one course of action, project, commitment, even life-plan, is to turn one's back on perhaps countless

---

[16] Ibid., p. 363.   [17] Ibid., p. 372.
[18] Ibid., pp. 349–50, 370 n. 2; on 'queerness', see p. 349 n. 1.

other opportunities of worthwhile action, project, commitment, life . . . How, then, can there be *right* and *wrong*
choices? How, indeed, can there be fully *practical* truth, i.e.
truth not merely in evaluation but in choice and action?
Here, I say, Wiggins falters. *Evaluations*, he conceded,
indeed contended, can have both objectivity and truth. To
practical judgments, on the other hand, he concedes objectivity
but not, perhaps, truth. Moreover, he insists on the importance of distinguishing between evaluation and practical
judgments. Yet he recognizes that there is what he calls a
'no-man's land' (really it is an overlap, and a challenge to
the distinction) between evaluation and practical judgment;
for some evaluations, e.g. of actions as ignoble or inhuman
or unspeakably wicked to do or not to do, bear directly on
action and offer themselves as conclusive practical judgments.[19] But how (Wiggins asks) are we to make such practical judgments, or any *true* practical judgments, when goods
are so plural and mutually irreducible?[20] Better and worse
practical judgments can be argumentatively distinguished,
though not always ordered; in that sense, at least, practical
judgments can have objectivity, and there can be practical
wisdom and unwisdom.[21] Perhaps, indeed, practical judgments
can have truth; but that (he thinks) is not clear. What is clear
to him is that their truth is not a matter of conformity to
any system of axioms or rules; the truth of practical judgments is just 'seen', by a 'situational appreciation' which can
be made only by the person judging.[22] Here Wiggins makes
his own a well-known strand of Aristotle's thought about
ethics. And he thinks the conceptual framework that we need
for practical judgment may be 'precisely what Aristotle
provides'.[23]

But ethics, I think, has made progress since Aristotle.
His ethical treatises were decidedly hazy about the starting points of practical reasoning. That is demonstrated by the
great squabble, between nineteenth- and twentieth-century

---

[19] Wiggins, 'Truth, Invention and the Meaning of Life', pp. 338-9, 370 n.2.
[20] Ibid., p. 368 esp. n. 1.
[21] Ibid., p. 372; Wiggins, 'Deliberation and Practical Reason' (1975-6) *Proceedings of the Aristotelian Society*, 29, reprinted in part in Joseph Raz (ed.),
Practical Reasoning (OUP: 1978) 144 at 146-7.
[22] Wiggins, in Raz, *Practical Reasoning* at pp. 147, 149.
[23] Ibid., p. 149.

exegetes, about whether Aristotle envisaged that ends, as well as means, are the subject of deliberation or even of *intelligent* identification. Today there are many (Allan, Gauthier, Mc-Dowell, Wiggins . . .) who rightly contend that Aristotle did envisage deliberation and intelligent identification of ends, i.e. of the ends which somehow constitute *eudaimonia*, a meaningful or flourishing life. But no one has much to say about what those ends might be. That is an issue on which progress was made, I think, by Aquinas. But such progress as was made was lost to view, because Aquinas did not carry through and consolidate his own advance.

His advance had been twofold. First, he repudiated the tendency of Aristotelian ethics to seek a single ultimate end which (given favourable circumstances) could be sufficiently participated in by individuals in their own terrestrial lifetimes. (That is not, of course, a tendency strongly in evidence amongst modern Aristotelians.) Secondly, he elaborated some implications of Aristotle's thought by sketching an identification of basic ends constitutive of human flourishing.

Aquinas comes at this identification in at least five distinct ways:

(i) The general object of one's will is intelligible good in general (and most radically that supremely intelligible good of knowing the creator, sustainer and director of all other goods); and within that general object are 'comprehended' and 'contained' ('like, so to speak, particular goods') those forms of good which are the ends not only of particular human capacities (as truth is the object of one's intelligence) but also of the whole person in his natural integrity (so that 'existence and life, etc.' are to be included in the list of basic natural goods).[24]

(ii) That list is expanded to something nearer its proper length when Aquinas argues that there is not one but a number of 'first principles' of practical reason (i.e. of natural law), all 'founded upon' the intelligibility of good as 'to be done and pursued (and the bad to be avoided)', and all therefore identifying goods to be done and pursued: here he lists life and its preservation; procreative union, education of children, 'and so forth'; knowledge of truth, especially about

[24] *Summa Theologiae*, I-II, q. 10, a. 1c.

ultimates; sociable living and communicating, 'and so forth'; and reasonableness in choosing, acting, living . . .[25]

(iii)   That last-mentioned good, the good of extending one's reasonableness into one's decisions and actions, is (when it is itself fully pursued and participated in) the disposition which we call the virtue of practical wisdom (*prudentia*), and that virtue provides the indispensable direction needed for all the other moral virtues. Practical wisdom itself gets its indispensable direction from those other basic principles, those principles which formulate one's understanding of the other basic goods and ends in the list (life, knowledge, sociability, etc. . . .).[26]

(iv)   Thus one's understanding of those most basic first principles is not itself an understanding of the moral principles needed to give guidance in the various 'fields and circumstances' of one's actual life; those first principles, understood just in themselves and without their moral implications, are not the principles which formulate the contours of a morally good life; rather they are only 'so to speak, the seeds of the virtues'.[27]

(v)   Thus, between those first principles and *moral* norms such as we find in, say, the Decalogue there is a logical space, which is filled by a process of 'derivation' or inference. The derivation or inference is in some cases immediate and obvious; but in others it requires wisdom, i.e. a reasonableness not found in everyone or even in most people.[28]

Here, then, is the gap which Aquinas failed to fill. His work was theology, not philosophical ethics. On the reasonable (but not philosophical) postulates of his theological method, the primary evidence for the particular *moral* principles and precepts which he discussed is the witness to them in the revelation transmitted by the Old and New Testaments as accepted in the apostolic Church. He seems to have felt no urgent need to carry through the philosophical explication of practical wisdom. That wisdom he himself identified as a twofold movement. There is the movement from goods and principles (of natural law) recognized by

---

[25] *ST* I–II, q. 94, aa. 2c, 3c.
[26] *ST* II–II, q. 47, a. 6c & ad 3; q. 47, a. 13 ad 2.
[27] *ST* I–II, q. 63, a. 1c; q. 51, a. 1c.
[28] *ST* I–II, q. 100, aa. 1c, 3c, 11c.

everyone to moral precepts (still of natural law) whose truth is accessible only to a wisdom not shared by all. And there is the movement from evaluations of possibilities as opportunities (true goods) to practical choices by individuals, choices which could have the objectivity of reasonableness without themselves being *uniquely* determined or required by any general principles or precepts.

The history of moral philosophy, especially in the centuries during which it has sought to distinguish its method from the method proper to theology, is the history of a search for the missing *intermediate principles*. This search for principles, to guide the transition from judgments about human goods to judgments about the right thing to do here and now, has been waylaid by all sorts of intellectual, spiritual and cultural confusions. Note particularly the unhappy tendency to find a spurious, or at best only partial, unity of ethical thought, by casting a single principle as the master principle or axiom from which all ethical conclusions are to be derived, or in terms of which all moral virtues are to be explained. Still, the list of failed candidates for this imagined role is a helpful checklist of 'intermediate principles' of the sort we are looking for. For a proper philosophical ethics, a useful assemblage of reminders is thus afforded by Kant, by the universalizing prescriptivists, by existentialist prophets of authenticity, by the ancient and modern Stoic proponents of detachment, and even by the utilitarians.

III.5   *'Right reason': the transparency of practical reasonableness*

Practical reasonableness is an opportunity. Being reasonable in one's choices, commitments, actions and habits is a form of life in which one can participate to a greater or lesser degree. In short, it is a good, indeed a basic good, neither reducible to nor superior or alternative to any of the other basic goods: life, knowledge, play, creativity, friendship . . .

Practical reasonableness makes its claims upon us because it is a basic aspect of human flourishing. Its claim is: to direct the way in which we seek to participate in each and all of the basic human goods. It is architectonic: directive, in charge . . . But its claim to be architectonic should not be explained in

Aristotle's fashion: viz., reason is what distinguishes us from other animals, so . . .; or again, more plausibly: reason (*nous*) is 'the best (or the highest) thing in us'.[29] Neither the metaphysical typology nor the metaphysical ranking is the sort of explanation we need in philosophical ethics; rather, they themselves, particularly the ranking, are to be explained as expressions and recognitions of the directive claims that our intelligence makes upon us *because of the goods (and other truths) which intelligence makes evident and thus available to us.*

What I have emphasized at the end of the preceding sentence is the transparency of reason. 'Transparency' is a metaphor intended here to help illuminate a range of important logical peculiarities clustered around the use of the first-person singular, present-tense. When these peculiarities are misunderstood, serious misunderstandings of reason and its activities are inevitable. As I have already mentioned (I.1 above), assertions such as 'I think that *p* (since . . .)' are transparent for assertions of the form 'It is the case that *p*' or, simply, '*p*'. Thus the 'I think' in assertions of the former kind is transparent for the real subject-matter of the assertion; my thinking is not part of that subject-matter at all; it is simply not the topic. (Of course it can be made, to some extent, a topic, as perhaps when someone says 'A penny for your thoughts', and you reply 'I am thinking about the fact that *p* . . .')

Before returning to the transparency of practical reasonableness, let me give an example of the way in which failure to take account of transparency can cause gross misunderstanding. A says to his adviser B, 'Can I rightly do X in such-and-such circumstances?' That is a question of conscience; but it is not a question *about* conscience. If B replies 'Those who in good faith (or: in conscience) believe that they can rightly do X do not sin in doing X', he has failed to answer the question and has answered a question which does not arise here and now for A. The question B has answered is the third-person question 'Would A be sinning if he did X, believing (rightly or wrongly) that he could rightly do X?' But A's question was the first-person question: 'Can I rightly believe

---

[29] *Nic. Eth.* X, 7: 1177a11-1178a9.

that I can rightly do X?'—and that, because of the transparency of the first person, is simply the following question, posed practically, i.e. for the purposes of deciding what to do: 'Is X right or wrong?' A is seeking to form his conscience; he is not asking what would be his culpability if he did X with a conscience formed and settled in a certain way. And this would be so even if he chose to frame his question thus: 'I have the following question of conscience: Can I rightly do X in such-and-such circumstances?' To repeat, a question *of* conscience is not a question *about* conscience or conscientiousness, any more than a statement of the form 'I think that *p*' is a statement about myself rather than about *p*.

We will meet transparency again, when discussing 'eventism' (better known as, for example, utilitarianism): see VI.1 below. The present importance of transparency is simply this: When we talk in ethics about practical reasonableness or 'right reason' *(recta ratio, orthos logos . . .)*, we must not be taken to suppose that practical reasonableness is the supreme good. Ethics is not just, or even particularly, for intellectuals or rationalists, for people who want to distinguish themselves from other animals, or people who want to cultivate a special ('the highest') part of their make-up. The point of being practically reasonable is not: being practically reasonable, full stop. Rather, it is: participating in all the human goods *well*. 'Well', here, expresses the implications not of some *further*, external (e.g. 'moral') standard, but simply of all those human goods to be participated in, integrally, in each and all of one's self-constitutive choices. The topic of assertions of the form 'Practical reasonableness requires that X should be done' is not practical reasonableness but X, doing X and one, some or all of the basic human goods, which make(s) doing X seem an intelligent and worthwhile thing to do.

Now when we are talking about human goods we are talking about 'perfections', aspects of human flourishing or fulfilment (see II.3, II.4 above). So we should say that the master principle of ethical reasoning is this: Make one's choices open to human fulfilment: i.e. avoid unnecessary limitation of human potentialities. None the less, it was not wrong for the classical theorists to say that the master principle is 'Follow [right] reason'; nor was Kant speaking foolishly when he said that the only unqualified good is the good will; nor am I contradicting myself when I say both that practical reasonableness is transparent for the human goods and that practical reasonableness is itself a basic human good. It was not wrong for the classical theorists to give pride of place to *recta ratio* and *orthos logos*: 'Be reasonable!' For our make-up as choosers and doers is complex. Feeling and emotion may conspire with intelligence and reasonableness, or they may compete with and undermine intelligence and reasonableness. Always I am liable to be deflected from pursuit of the understood good into pursuit of the good which promises me some satisfactions, here and now, for me. Attaining a harmony of one's emotions with one's understanding and reason, and even more importantly a harmony between one's practical judgments and decisions and one's actual actions, is not something accomplished by nature. It is a good, to be understood and cultivated. Though, like the other basic goods, it can be instrumental and indeed is distinctive in being always somehow instrumental to one's participation in one or more of the other basic goods, its significance is not at all exhausted by its utility. It is itself a basic form of human fulfilment. So I do not contradict myself when I stress both the transparency of practical reasonableness (in so far as it is one's guide to participation in human goods), and the not-merely-instrumental human goodness of practical reasonableness itself (as the realization of the human potentiality for inner integration and outer authenticity).

There remains my point about Kant. 'Nothing in the world', he says, '—indeed nothing even beyond the world— can possibly be conceived which could be called good without qualification except a *good will*'.[30] Now by 'will', as Kant says, he means 'nothing more than practical reason': 'the will is a faculty of choosing only that which reason, independently of inclination, recognizes as practically necessary, i.e. as good'.[31] So there is much good sense, as well as some exaggeration, some equivocation, and some impoverishment,

---

[30] Kant, *Grundlegung zur Metaphysik der Sitten* [1785], First Section (Prussian Academy edn, vol. IV (Berlin: 1911), 392-3; trans. Beck (R. P. Wolff, ed.), *Foundations of the Metaphysics of Morals* (Bobbs-Merrill, Indianapolis: 1969), p. 11.   [31] Ibid., Second Section, 412; trans. Beck, p. 34.

in what Kant says. There is impoverishment to the extent that Kant's understanding of understanding (reason) overlooks the *intelligible* goodness of the specific, substantive aspects of human flourishing, and seeks to make do with reason's 'a priori' power of universalizing. There is equivocation to the extent that practical reason is properly 'independent' of inclination only in attending to the *object* of inclination rather than to the sheer fact that 'I have an urge to . . .'; practical reason itself, however, is the working out of an inclination (with an object, practical reasonableness [as transparent for . . .]), and the goods it is concerned with *are* the objects of characteristic human inclinations. There is, finally, exaggeration in Kant to the extent that he makes practical reasonableness not only an intrinsic 'good in itself', and the 'condition of every other good', but also ' the supreme good'.[32]

Yet we must do Kant justice; he recognizes that practical reasonableness is 'not the sole and complete good'.[32] If we bear that in mind, we can read everything he says about good will as a strenuous insistence, only slightly askew, on the *architectonic* role of practical reasonableness.

That role is best understood, however, when we acknowledge what Kant overlooked: reason's *transparency* for all the goods. All those goods come together in a good life, or, more accurately, in a good person (the embodiment of Kant's 'good will'), if but only if they are participated in by way of reasonable choices, projects, commitments—for only through such choices is the goodness of each and all of the basic goods both respected and fostered.

III.6   *The variety of intermediate principles and the argument from relativity*

Ordinary 'moral principles', about murder, stealing, promise-keeping, calumny, and so on, can be reached by arguments which start from one or more of the intermediate principles and have as their middle term one or other of the basic human goods. That is why I have called these intermediate principles the *basic* requirements of practical reasonableness.

I have argued elsewhere that there are eight or nine basic

---

[32] *Grundlegung*, First Section, 396; trans. Beck p. 15.

OBJECTIVITY, TRUTH AND MORAL PRINCIPLES   75

requirements of practical reasonableness.[33] The first three
respond to the multiplicity of basic goods, of opportunities
of participating in them, of persons who can participate in
them . . .: (1) have a harmonious set of orientations, purposes
and commitments; (2) do not leave out of account, or arbitrarily discount or exaggerate, any of the basic human goods;
(3) do not leave out of account, or arbitrarily discount or
exaggerate, the goodness of other people's participation in
human goods. The next two respond to the emotional pull
of immoderate and one-eyed enthusiasm and of apathy,
inertia, laziness . . .: (4) do not attribute to any particular
project the overriding and unconditional significance which
only a basic human good and a general commitment can
claim; (5) pursue one's general commitments with creativity
and do not abandon them lightly. The next calls for more
than mere well-meaning and good intentions: (6) do not
waste your opportunities by using needlessly inefficient
methods, and do not overlook the foreseeable bad consequences of your choices. (The irrational extrapolation of
this requirement into utilitarian or proportionalist or consequentialist rationalizations is the topic of Chapter IV.)
The next is the requirement insisted upon by St Paul and, as
the second formulation of his categorical imperative, by
Kant; I formulate it thus: (7) do not choose directly against
any basic human good (the theme of Chapter V). The next
acknowledges that the human goods are realized and protected by, *inter alia*, the actions of groups and of group
members acting as such: (8) foster the common good of
your communities. The last of the requirements that I listed
in my book responds to the problem of extending reasonable
judgment into reasonable choice, in the face of conformism
and other temptations: (9) do not act contrary to your
conscience, i.e. against your best judgment about the implications for your own action of these requirements of practical
reasonableness and the moral principles they generate or
justify.

To those I would now add another, suggested by reflection
on the experience machine (II.3): do not choose apparent
goods, knowing them to be only the simulations of real goods,

---

[33] *Natural Law and Natural Rights*, ch. V.

even when the simulation brings real emotions or experiences, real satisfactions.

It will be apparent that these requirements are expressions of the most general moral principle—that one remain open to integral human fulfilment—in the various normative and existential contexts in which choice must respond to that most general principle. Hence the evident overlap between many of the requirements. Hence, too, the possibility of other formulations or other intermediate principles, as other contexts or sets of contexts are considered. Germain Grisez's most recent work, for example, shows how the list of requirements would look if it were systematically conceived as a set of norms for securing reasonableness against the distortions introduced into choice by the demands of emotion, feeling, and the like. On this basis, for example, the requirement that basic goods be respected in every act would be bifurcated; for a choice against a basic good can be motivated on the one hand by hatred, vengefulness, anger and the like, and on the other hand by positive desire to secure some other form of good or the same good in another instance.

Let me leave the details of systematizing the intermediate principles of moral thought and turn, finally, to the second of the moral sceptic's master arguments. The first was the argument from queerness (III.1 above). The second is the argument from the historical, geographical, anthropological *variety* of moral rules and cultures. John Mackie called it 'the argument from relativity'. It 'has as its premiss', he said, 'the well-known variation in moral codes from one society to another and from one period to another, and also the differences in moral beliefs between different groups and classes within a complex community'.[34]

The wide popularity of this argument in modern culture (prefigured by its popularity in the culture of late Antiquity) is unimpressive because so often unreflective. Proper attention to the historical and anthropological data shows that the basic forms of human good, and the corresponding practical principles, are recognized, by human beings, both in thought and action, with virtual universality, in all times and places. Proper reflection on the complex structure of practical reasonableness

---

[34] Mackie, *Ethics*, p. 36.

—with the various intermediate quasi-methodological principles mediating between the basic practical principles and
fully specific moral norms—suggests that inter-personal and
cultural variation in formulation and recognition of moral
norms is just what would be expected. Though the many
intermediate principles are themselves expressed or implied
in many proverbial forms in very many cultures, the fact
remains that an imperfect grasp of even one of them will
distort practical reasonableness across a whole range of
moral norms. And then the ingenuity of human intelligence
is readily available to disguise the imperfection and distortion with rationalizations that block truly rational critique
for generations, eras, whole civilizations.

Because full-blown ethical reasoning is itself practical (I.1
above), the intelligence and reasonableness which yield
ethical conclusions have to operate on and within the very
material (desires, impulses, aversions . . .) which are the
source of the biases which threaten all intellectual activity.
Inevitably, therefore, it is more difficult to be reasonable and
objective in ethics (and the other *practical* disciplines) than in
science, mathematics and logic. To assert that objectivity is
therefore impossible is a mere (gross) fallacy, an open defiance
of logic.

I do not suggest that all moral variations and differences
are the upshot of deficiency in practical reasonableness. Here,
as elsewhere, the sceptic is a disappointed absolutist, and we
must reject the sophistical dilemma, 'all or nothing'. In particular, we must beware the (often unconscious) legalism
which supposes that if there is no *uniquely correct* solution
to a moral problem, no solution to that problem is objectively
right (or wrong). The language of 'right' and 'wrong' must
not lure us into assuming that for every problem or situation
there is one solution or choice which is *the* right one. As I
shall later explain (IV.2), vast areas of individual and social
choice require commitments which, before they are made,
are not *determined* by any or all of the requirements of
practical reasonableness but which, once they are made, do
tend to determine specific moral norms, standards and obliga-
tions which would not have existed (in those specific forms,
if at all) but for those commitments.

Relative to the legalistic ideal of 'one right answer', the

moral choice of many basic commitments is *underdetermined*; as Wiggins says, 'cognitively underdetermined'.[35] But it does not at all follow that even the cognitively underdetermined choices are arbitrary inventions which could just as well have taken any form whatsoever. Nor does it follow that all choices are in any sense cognitively underdetermined. In tolerating the suggestion that they are, and in suggesting that practical judgments and choices, unlike evaluations, cannot be true-in-virtue-of-the-way-the-world-is,[36] Wiggins forgets his own recognition that 'between pure valuations and pure directives [i.e. practical judgments or choices]' there are 'general or particular statements about actions which it is ignoble or inhuman or unspeakably wicked to do or not to do'.[37] He gives no reason to suppose that these statements, which provide very determinate and immediate guidance for choices, lack the objectivity and truth which he himself rightly allows to 'pure evaluations' (III.3 above). Nor does he give reason to doubt that some of these statements express principles or norms; but if so, there is no reason to accept his claim that the truth of a concrete practical judgment (e.g. 'I ought not to do X to this woman because that would be killing the innocent, directly violating the basic good of life') does not consist (even in part?) in its conformity to an 'axiom or rule'. In Chapter V, I seek to show how such practical judgments have their truth at least in part in their conformity to one or more of the 'intermediate principles' of practical reasonableness.

NOTES

III.3

Locke on the non-objectivity of 'secondary qualities' . . . See *An Essay concerning Human Understanding* [1690], Book II, ch. viii, sec. 25. For the related theses of Hume and Mackie in ethics, see Mackie, *Ethics*, pp. 19–20; Mackie, *Hume's Moral Theory*, pp. 58–9.

Scientistic conceptions of the world and of objectivity . . . See John McDowell, 'Are Moral Requirements Hypothetical Imperatives?' (1978) *Proc. Aris. Soc., Supp. Vol.* 52, 13 at p. 19: '. . . world views richer

---

[35] Wiggins, 'Truth, Invention and the Meaning of Life', p. 366; cf. pp. 368–75.
[36] Ibid., p. 370.   [37] Ibid., pp. 338–9.

than that of science are not scientific, but not on that account unscientific (a term of opprobium for answers other than those of science to science's questions). To query their status as world views on the ground of their not being scientific is to be motivated not by science but by scientism.' Likewise Wiggins, 'Truth and Interpretation' at p. 46. See also Eric Voegelin, 'The Origins of Scientism' (1948) 15 *Social Research* 462-94.

III.4

The irreducibly and equally basic forms of human good . . . See Finnis, *Natural Law and Natural Rights*, ch. VI. 4. Note: to say that the basic forms of human good are all equally basic is not at all to say that a life can *just as well* be organized around any one of them as around any of the others; the basic goods are not all equally architectonic.

III.5

The transparency of conscience . . . see also Alan Donagan, *The Theory of Morality* (University of Chicago Press, Chicago and London: 1977), pp. 136-8.

III.6

Germain Grisez on the intermediate principles of practical reasonableness . . . For his earlier treatments of what he calls the modes of responsibility, see bibliography in Finnis, *Natural Law and Natural Rights*, p. 129. For his most recent treatment, see Grisez, *The Way of the Lord Jesus: A Summary of Catholic Moral Theology*, Volume One, *Christian Moral Principles* (Franciscan Herald Press, Chicago: 1983), ch. 7.

Anthropological evidence of variety in moral cultures . . . See the discussion and bibliography in Finnis, *Natural Law and Natural Rights*, pp. 81-5, 97. For the sceptical (mis)use of this evidence in late Antiquity, see e.g. Sextus Empiricus, *Hypotyposes [Outlines of Pyrrhonism]* [c.200], Book I, 145-63.

IV
Utilitarianism, Consequentialism, Proportionalism . . . or Ethics?

IV.1 *The varieties and the terminology*

Scepticism about human goods, including the good of practical reasonableness, was the main concern of the preceding chapters. In the next two chapters, and more, I focus on the threat to ethics posed by the ideas usually labelled 'utilitarianism', 'consequentialism', or 'proportionalism'. Scepticism was well known to the ancients; as doctrines, utilitarianism and the like were not.

The critique I shall develop is valid, I believe, for all versions of these doctrines or devices of ethical reasoning. Those whose opinions I criticize often reply that theirs is not a utilitarianism but a consequentialism; or not a consequentialism but a proportionalism; or not a proportionalism but a teleological ethics . . .; or is simply not to be labelled at all. So we must be able to state each opinion without using any of these labels. But we are entitled to *stipulate* how we use such-and-such a label, in our own critique. The label we stipulate should approximate to its ordinary uses. So the ordinary philosophical uses of these labels can usefully be reviewed; that will remind us, too, of the range of opinions in question. After making a brief review of terminology, I will stipulate my own use of the one label which, simply for expository convenience, I shall thereafter use to signify the whole range of opinions in question.

A. *'Utilitarianism'*

'Utilitarianism' is the most common philosophical label for those opinions. For it was the English utilitarians who launched this genre of ethical reasoning. 'Utility' is, of course, an ethical term of much greater antiquity and of much wider and less specific use. But the utility the utilitarians had in mind is the aptness of an action (or omission) to produce the state of experience called 'pleasure', 'satisfaction' or 'happiness'. Their theory was that the right act, the act which ought to be done, is the act which will (or will probably) maximize that agreeable state of experience; that, then, is the act of greatest utility. Their theoretical strategy was later to be generalized: postulate some good as the human good and then seek to identify the act which will maximize that good; that act is (by definition) the act of greatest utility and (by ethical stipulation) the right act. It is easy to see how people came to use the term 'utility' as it is used in much contemporary discussion, especially theoretical economics: viz. as the purely formal concept of a 'that which is to be (ought to be) maximized', i.e. a maximand.

Hedonistic utilitarianism and eudaemonistic utilitarianism are nowadays commonly disowned by utilitarians, who grant that those conceptions of the maximand are indeed extremely impoverished accounts of human good(s). But utilitarians who notice this impoverishment confront a parting of the ways. Some seek to combine the strategy of maximizing with an enriched and more adequate conception of basic human goods. This is the way followed by a good many of those working in Catholic theology during the past fifteen years (for no theology identifying pleasure or experiential 'happiness' as *the* substantial human goods can plausibly claim to be Christian). As we shall see, this way soon runs into a dead-end.

Philosophers who wish to retain the strategy of aggregating and maximizing have therefore preferred, generally, the other way. Instead of enriching the conception of the good to be maximized, they dilute the maximand still further: it becomes, simply, whatever is desired; or, more commonly nowadays, the realization or satisfaction of 'preferences'. Thus William James in America and Bertrand Russell in England proposed a utilitarianism which postulates that every desire of every person has an equal claim to satisfaction. This is the theoretical core of the social engineering proposed by Roscoe Pound and a whole American school of pragmatist jurists and political theorists. It obviously has methodological affinities with John Rawls's principle that a theory of the goods to be distributed in a society must be a 'thin theory' because any richer account of basic goods would be undemocratic (II.6 above). But attention to the destructiveness and folly of many *desires* tarnishes the attractions of the Jamesian postulate. Hence we get a revised version: maximize the realization or satisfaction of *preferences*, i.e. of rational (in some suitably restricted sense of 'rational') choices. The attractions of this preference utilitarianism in the face of obvious and overwhelming difficulties (IV.2 below) owe something, I think, to the prestige, in our civilization, of the act of choice, the exercise of free will. (This, if my speculation be correct, is one of several ways in which utilitarianism is a residue of Christianity: see also IV.3, V.1). At the same time, part of the attraction of the term 'preference' is that it can hover between (uncriticized) desires and (intelligent, or rational) choice.

B. *'Consequentialism'*

The trouble with the label 'utilitarianism' is that, for the historical reasons I have sketched, it savours strongly of certain particular and dubious conceptions of the maximand. In an effort to direct attention towards other features of the strategy, G. E. M. Anscombe introduced the term 'consequentialism'.[1] She was wanting to focus, not on the maximand, but on the strategy of 'maximizing', and in particular on the postulate that one is responsible for *all* the expected consequences, whether intended or unintended, of one's choices and should therefore choose so as to optimize those consequences. I now shift from 'maximize' to 'optimize' to mark the fact that classical utilitarianism has to decide whether to maximize goods such as pleasure or 'happiness', or to *minimize* evils such as pain or misery. On the assumption that pleasures and pains are commensurable and can therefore be netted, one can retain the term 'maximize' in one's account of the general strategy. But that assumption is extremely questionable. To draw a veil, therefore, over all such problems (and over the other problems of commensuration of maximands: IV.2), I use the optimistic notion of 'optimizing' consequences. Consequentialists, then, are those who propose that optimizing the consequences of one's

[1] G. E. M. Anscombe, 'Modern Moral Philosophy' (1958) 33 *Philosophy* 1; also in *Collected Philosophical Papers of G. E. M. Anscombe* (Blackwell, Oxford: 1981), vol. III, at p. 36.

choices is either the supreme principle of ethics or a general principle always available to resolve 'hard cases'.

Many ethical theorists who are consequentialist in the sense just stipulated protest at being so labelled. Firstly, they may complain that the principle of optimizing consequences is not the only or even the supreme principle of their ethics; they object to being lumped together with those for whom it is. They wish to be regarded as 'mixed' or 'moderate' consequentialists. But, as we shall see (IV.3), to introduce a consequentialist principle into one's ethics, at any point—say, to resolve 'hard cases'—is to introduce an element of arbitrariness and rationalization which must consume the moralist's non-consequentialist principles unless he makes a further and also arbitrary *decision*, of the form 'Thus far and no further . . . at present'.

Secondly, they may object that it is not merely the value of the *consequences* of an action that they seek to optimize; they wish to include in their computations of overall value the intrinsic value of the action itself, at least in some cases. This objection can be accepted, so far as it goes. It does not touch my objections to consequentialism. I am quite content that the value of the action itself be taken into account along with the value of its consequences; for indeed, the action itself (the item of behaviour) can be regarded as *the first consequence* of the *decision* whose rightness or wrongness is in question. But thus 'taking into account' the 'value of the action itself' will only compound the problem of incommensurability which, as we shall see (IV.2), renders the computation not merely impracticable but actually senseless.

Lastly, it is sometimes objected that no clear line can be drawn between an action and its consequences. But the fact remains that, however the line be drawn, there are consequences of decisions and actions, and consequentialists tell us *never* to fail to evaluate *all* these (actual or foreseeable) consequences. That injunction is quite distinctive, and is open to objections which would be valid even if the distinction between actions and their consequences were as difficult, arbitrary or theoretically impossible as they claim.

Utilitarianism is a form of consequentialism. Consequentialism is the wider category, and affords in that respect a more convenient label. But if we use it, we need to remind our

listeners that we are not overlooking the value which a consequentialist of a certain sort attributes to some actions 'in
themselves'. Moreover, our listeners need to be reminded
that when we reject consequentialism as irrational, we are
not in the least proposing that sound ethical reasoning
ignores or systematically discounts consequences. On the
contrary, a basic requirement of practical reasonableness
is that one attend to likely consequences of one's decisions.
That basic requirement was plainly stated and explained in
Chapter V. 6 of my *Natural Law and Natural Rights*. But
since Chapter V. 7 elaborated a severe critique of *consequen-*
tialism, some have said that I treat consequences as of no
account. This misunderstanding makes me now reluctant to
use the label.

C. *'Teleological ethics'*

This label is often favoured by utilitarians or consequentialists who dislike both the narrow historic connotations of
'utilitarian', and the fact that the label 'consequentialist'
was brought into use by opponents of their method and thus
savours of opprobrium. It is also rather favoured by Con-
tinental philosophers and theologians and their Anglo-Saxon
followers. For it recalls the grand modern bifurcation of
ethics into 'teleological' and 'deontological': the ethics of
ends and the ethics of duty. That dichotomy, however, fails
to accommodate Platonic, Aristotelian, Thomistic and any
other substantially reasonable ethics. For the moral terms,
'right' and 'wrong', *'duty'*, 'obligation', 'vice' and 'virtue',
and so forth, express the *requirements* of practical reasonableness, but those requirements are nothing but the implications of an integral pursuit of the basic forms of human
good (including the good of practical reasonableness itself)
which constitute the basic *ends* of all rational decision and
action: III.5 above. Ethics is thoroughly deontological; the
basic practical principles which express the basic forms of
human good are not, in themselves, moral or ethical principles. But ethics is also thoroughly teleological; all specific
moral norms identifying duties, etc., are derived (via the
intermediate principles which I call requirements of practical
reasonableness: III.6) from the basic practical principles
identifying intelligible objects (ends) of human pursuit.

So 'teleology', with or without prefixes such as 'mixed' or 'moderate', labels utilitarian or consequentialist or other like methods only vaguely and with a *suggestio falsi*.

D. *'Proportionalism'*

This is a label recently introduced by theologians who wish to assert or imply a historical continuity between a 'principle of proportionality' used for centuries in Catholic ethical theory and their own utilitarian or consequentialist methodology (which in some cases is 'pure', i.e. architectonic, supreme, exclusive, and in other cases is proposed as 'mixed' or 'moderate' because used only to resolve 'hard cases' or 'conflict situations').

The supposed historical continuity is very questionable. The historic 'principle of proportionality', as an explicit principle in ethical theory, was launched by Aquinas in distinguishing between murder and self-defence by the argument of 'double effect'. 'An act done with a good intention', says Aquinas, 'can be rendered morally bad by being *disproportionate* to its end [si non sit proportionatus fini]'. But, as the sentence just quoted implies and the succeeding sentence[2] confirms, the proportionality in question is no more than the proportion of a specific means to a specific end: if stunning one's assailant will suffice for self-defence, one must not shoot him through the heart; that would not be 'proportionate', and the choice to inflict needless harm would be immoral. There is here no trace of any doctrine that it is morally permissible to kill when one considers that the good to be attained by killing outweighs (is proportionately greater than) the harms created overall by killing and the goods to be attained overall by not killing. Nor is any such doctrine to be found in the other passages of Aquinas where recent theologians have claimed to find it.

Notwithstanding its factitious historical associations, the term 'proportionalism' has some advantages as a label for the range of utilitarian, consequentialist and other like ethical methodologies. It avoids any suggestion that every such methodology must work with an implausible maximand such

---

[2] 'And so if someone, in order to defend his own life, uses more violence than is necessary [ad defendendum propriam vitam utatur majori violentia quam oporteat], his act is immoral': *ST* II–II, q. 64, a. 7c.

as *utility* (conceived as a state of consciousness). It avoids an *apparent* connotation of the label 'consequentialist', that the benefits and harms inherent in the chosen act itself are to be ignored. Moreover, it embraces all those methods which offer to determine right choice by reference to *quantities* of benefit and harm, not merely those methods which insist on *maximization* of benefit. For one is a proportionalist if one offers to identify the morally right choice as the one that will bring about a *better proportion of benefits to harms* than any other available choice. Given a sufficiently relaxed notion of benefits and harms, we can therefore say that all forms of utilitarianism and consequentialism are forms of proportionalism.

So now I shall speak of proportionalism where in earlier writings I have spoken of consequentialism. I shall use the label that has been chosen by proponents, not opponents, of the doctrines I criticize—proponents, moreover, who usually subscribe to a theory of objective basic goods very similar to the theory I defend. (Remember: there are countless proportionalists who have never even heard of that label!)

But I must acknowledge a disadvantage of the label. Appeals to 'proportionality', as a criterion of moral judgment, are to be found in authors who are not proportionalists. An appeal to proportionality is not proportionalist if it expresses some *prior* moral judgment or assessment, or refers to the implications of some prior commitment *relative to which* a proposed choice would be proportionate (fitting, appropriate . . .) or disproportionate (unfitting, inappropriate . . .). *There is proportionalism only where an assessment of overall benefits and harms, not dependent on any other moral judgment, is made the exclusive criterion of moral judgment, or the criterion for overriding or qualifying other moral judgments.*

IV.2   *Incommensurability*

In all its forms, proportionalism claims that basic moral direction is afforded by the following methodological injunction:

> Compare the benefits and harms promised by alternative possible choices (whether the choice be of commitment to

rules or ways of life, or of a one-off action), and make that
choice which promises to yield a better proportion of
benefit to harm than any available alternative choice.

Note that 'better proportion' here relates to *quantities* of
value, not to better and worse as measured by some independent moral standard. As I have just said, proportionalism offers to provide basic, not derivative, moral direction
(either for all choices or for choices in 'hard cases'). Similarly,
I use the term 'harm' not to imply some crude or restricted
(e.g. physicalist) conception of the elements to be compared,
but simply to avoid any 'already moralized' connotations of
the word 'evil': 'harm' can be read as pain, loss, defect, non-
realization of preference . . .

Thus, 'better proportion' can be read as, say, 'maximum
net good' or 'minimum net harm'. Here, 'maximum' need not
refer to any abstractly conceivable or cardinally computable
sum; it may simply mean 'more than any alternative'. The
proportionalist computation can be ordinal, not (as in
classical utilitarianism) cardinal; it seeks the optimum outcome and thus the optimific choice.

Alternatively, as we shall see (IV.5), 'better [or worse] proportion' can be read as proposing a more restricted computation, e.g. of the long-term overall net harm to one basic
'pre-moral' form of human good, by way of harm to another
different but associated basic good.

In any case, what is proposed is a computation. And the
injunction to undertake it is not just impracticable but is
actually senseless. It is senseless in the way that it is senseless
to try to sum up the quantity of the size of this page, the
quantity of the weight of this book, and the quantity of the
number six. At first glance, the computation seems possible;
after all, each of those quantities *is* a quantity, and thus has
in common with the others the feature that, of it, one can
sensibly ask: How much? Yet, on reflection, it is clear that
the different kinds of quantity—volume, weight, and cardinal
numbers—are objectively incommensurable. Of course, we
can *adopt* a system of weights and measures that will *bring*
the three kinds of quantity into a relation with each other;
the relations will differ radically according to the systems
adopted (metric, imperial, avoirdupois . . .). But adopting

systems of weights and measures is *nothing like* carrying out a computation in terms of the systems. And prior to the adoption, an instruction to compute is not merely impracticable; it is senseless.

The computations proposed by the early utilitarians, the Benthamites, were utterly impracticable but did not, in principle, suffer from the type of senselessness I am now concerned with. They were utterly impracticable because the total or overall consequences of actions are simply not foreseeable, even in terms of probability. Even if practicable, they would be exposed to all manner of objections against their use as the basis for moral judgment of choices. And in any case, they may well have been senseless for a reason which I shall not here consider: for if determinism is true, there are no alternative actions one could perform on a given occasion and so the best *possible* action is the action one actually performs; but if determinism is not true (i.e. persons have free choice) there simply is no such thing as 'the totality of what will happen if one decides in a certain way'.[3] But the point I want to make about the classical utilitarian proposals is that they did not suffer from the senselessness entailed by the incommensurability of human goods, for the computation they proposed was of a single, allegedly homogeneous common factor: pleasure, conceived as a quantifiable sensation.

But the pleasure theory of value has had to be abandoned for other reasons. Pleasures are not all or even mainly sensations, still less quantifiable sensations. Moreover, it is quite implausible to treat pain as commensurable with pleasure (as if they were lower and higher points on a single scale of value/disvalue); but unless they are so commensurable, there must be a choice between 'maximize pleasures' and 'minimize pains', and grounds for such a choice are not evident. (Anyone who tells you to 'Maximize good *and* minimize evil'[4] has simply failed to advert to a point made forcefully enough by Cicero,[5] and can never have seriously tried *using* his own

---

[3] See A. N. Prior, 'The Consequences of Actions', in his *Papers on Time and Tense* (OUP, Oxford: 1968), 51-8 at p. 52.

[4] For example, Timothy O'Connell, *Principles for a Catholic Morality* (Seabury Press, New York: 1978), 223 (where he calls it 'Schüller's Preference Principle'). Likewise R. M. Hare, *Moral Thinking*, p. 62 ('. . . as much good, and as little harm, as possible').

[5] Cicero, *De Finibus* II, 6-25, esp. 17; see also Robinson A. Grover, 'The

'method'.) Again, the notion that pleasure, in any sense, is the point of everything is absurd (but unless it were the point of everything, the injunction to maximize pleasures could not provide the basic moral direction). I need not now repeat all the results of the thought-experiment with the experience machine (II.3).

But as soon as one's account of the various basic aspects of human well-being has been made less naive than the Benthamites', the proportionalist computation becomes not only utterly impracticable but also senseless. For it proposes to compare incommensurables: the basic human goods are all equally and irreducibly basic; none of them is subordinated as mere means to any of the others. And that incommensurability is compounded by a further incommensurability; for the basic human goods are not abstract entities but aspects of the *being* of persons each of whom is distinct from and no mere means to the well-being of any other person.

Of course, it is possible to envisage two states of affairs, such that the one is rich in human goods and the other is devoid of such goods; say, a happy village and the same village buried under an earthquake. But proportionalism is not offered as an evaluation of alternative states of affairs, abstracted from their causes and aftermath. It is offered as a guide to the bringing-about of states of affairs by morally significant choices between intelligibly choosable alternative courses of action. And it instructs one to make right choices and avoid wrong choices. But, on the proportionalist explanations of 'right' and 'wrong', wrong choice would be not merely wrong but unintelligible and, as a *choice*, impossible. One can choose only what appears to one to be good; but if, as proportionalists claim, (i) 'wrong' entails 'yielding (or promising) less good', and (ii) there are choices which can be identified as yielding (or promising) less good than some alternative choice(s), then it becomes inconceivable that a *morally* wrong (as distinct from a merely mistaken) choice could ever be made. How could anyone *choose* an act which he can see yields less good than some alternative open to him? Morally wrong choices are, of course, unreasonable. But unreasonable choices are possible precisely because the goods apparently realizable by choices are *not* commensurable as yielding (or promising) greater or lesser good; they retain their attractiveness as yielding (or promising) some real good, an attractiveness which would be destroyed if that could be seen to embody or promise less good, all things considered, than some available alternative. The unreasonableness of morally wrong choices is not the incomprehensibility of choosing a lesser good. Rather it is the unreasonableness of pursuing good arbitrarily, or unfairly, or fanatically, or in-constantly, or by means of a direct attack on some basic good, or in some other way contrary to a principle of practical reasonableness.

Notice, incidentally, that the tradition of ethics has always known the maxim which Cicero formulates as *minima de malis eligenda*,[6] choose the lesser of evils. But the tradition never supposed that this is an expression or application of a proportionalist principle or methodology. The maxim had, and has, a particular meaning and a restricted application: if you are determined to act unreasonably, do not go the whole hog—if you are set on wrongdoing, at least restrict your wrong; the less serious your wrongdoing, the better. This is not an invitation to decide what is and is not wrong-doing by means of an evaluation of predicted states of affairs (results, outcomes, consequences . . .) yielding more, or less, good overall.

IV.3   *How we evaluate practical solutions as 'better' or 'worse'*

But don't we, as individuals and as societies, have some stable and intelligent relative evaluations of solutions to practical (moral) problems as 'better' and 'worse' solutions? Indeed we do. Just as we adopt systems of weights and measures in terms of which we can *then* carry out commensurations, comparisons and computations of quantities, so we as individuals and societies adopt sets of commitments that *bring* the basic human values into a relation with each other suffi-cient to enable us to choose projects and, in some cases, to undertake a cost–benefit analysis to identify better and worse (and even, sometimes, best) solutions. And the adopting

[6] Cicero, *de Officiis* III, 28.

of such a basic set of commitments is, in fact, *nothing like* carrying out a computation of commensurable goods—not even the relatively restricted computation required for a merely ordinal comparison of the 'overall' good of alternative courses of action and their consequences.

This is not to say that the adopting of basic commitments is that 'choosing of basic values' which some contemporary sceptics make the basis of all practical reasoning and 'ethics'. On the contrary, basic values can be identified by intelligence, and as thus identified provide the principles of all choices however basic. Basic commitments shape our response to, our participation in, basic values—in the form of choices of career, of marriage, of forms of education, of preference for wealth as against leisure or liturgy, or for speed of communication as against safety.

The making of basic commitments is not arbitrary, directionless or indiscriminate. It is mere technocratic illusion to suppose that a choice not guided by cost–benefit computations must be arbitrary. On the contrary, the adoption of basic commitments is to be guided by all the requirements of practical reasonableness. The commitments must be stable and harmonious. They must give some place to each of the basic aspects of human well-being. They must not discount or exaggerate the goodness of any individual person's participation in human goods. No good should be accorded overriding, unconditional, exclusive significance. Each must be pursued creatively and with constancy. No choice may involve the direct suppression of any basic aspect of the well-being of any person . . . Do these seem vague? Try the thought-experiment of choosing basic commitments in a way which defies or ignores one (any one) of these requirements and you will see how much direction they give.

The range of rational application of cost–benefit computations, which proportionalists take as the model and method of ethical reasoning, is really very restricted. (Clearheaded economists are well aware of this restrictedness.) If we have decided to build a highway through the desert from A to B, we can use cost–benefit computations to select among materials and methods of levelling and road-building. But it was not, and could not rationally have been, cost–benefit computations which guided our prior commitment to the level of economic activity (trade) and personal mobility which calls for highways of this sort. We know that the building and use of highways of this sort involves the death of tens of thousands of persons, and the horrible injury of hundreds of thousands more, each year. But we have not made any computation which shows that the goods participated in and attained by that level of trade and mobility exceed, outweigh, are proportionately greater, than the goods destroyed and damaged by that level, or any level, of deaths and injuries. Nor, on the other hand, could any computation yield the conclusion that the deaths and injuries are an evil which objectively outweighs, exceeds, etc., the good of mobility, etc.

And these computations are impossible not merely because of the large numbers of persons and events in question. There would still be an impossibility in principle, i.e. an incoherence or senselessness by reason of incommensurability of goods, if you set out to *measure* the goods to be attained by yourself by a lifetime of travelling on highways and other dangerous transportation systems, in order to compare them with the harms/costs/evils to be avoided by yourself by a lifetime (perhaps much longer) of abstaining from all such dangerous means of transportation. Uncertainty of empirical outcomes is not the point in issue (though it is of much greater importance than proportionalist method allows for). For there is the very same impossibility of computing goods when we compare the completed lives of our hermit and our traveller.

Of course, we can often say which lifetime we would prefer. We have often made commitments *in terms of which* one life can be assessed as appropriate and successful and the other as deficient and regrettable. My point is simply that those commitments cannot be justified, even in principle, by proportionalist method. The justification, and equally the critique, of any basic commitment must be in terms of the requirements of practical reasonableness, which give positive direction even though they do not include any principle of optimizing (i.e. of ordinal maximizing), and even though they permit indefinitely many different commitments (as well as, also, excluding indefinitely many other possible commitments!).

The fact that basic commitments are made, both individually and socially, and that they provide the framework for vast numbers of everyday decisions and projects, and for the technical, financial, economic, accounting, cost-benefit analysis of so many options, is the reason why it can *seem* plausible to say, as proportionalists do, that moral problems (or some moral problems) can be resolved by the maxim 'choose the lesser evil'. Proportionalism persuades because its methodological maxim seems *self-evident*. Take Richard McCormick's appeal to a 'rule of reason', viz. 'Choose the lesser evil':

> This general statement is, it would seem, beyond debate; for the only alternative is that in conflict situations we should choose the greater evil, which is patently absurd.[7]

The fallacy should now be evident. The 'alternatives' envisaged by McCormick are not exhaustive. Indeed, they are not even available. The rational alternative to trying to choose the lesser evil is not: Choose the greater evil. It is to recognize that, in more-than-merely-technical problems ('conflict situations'), there is, really, *no* measurable 'greater' and 'lesser' evil (or good) at stake; that choice must therefore be guided by the genuine requirements of practical reasonableness.

The fallacious plausibility of proportionalism is greatly enhanced by its secret, often unconscious, legalism (cf. III.6 above): its assumption that there is a uniquely correct moral answer (or specifiable set of correct moral answers) to all genuine moral problems. This assumption spurs on the search for a method capable, at least 'in principle' (as they are fond of saying, with an eye to problems of computation which they, wrongly, think are caused only by human limitations), of yielding that answer, by reference to 'most (or more) goods' or 'least (or lesser) evils' or 'maximum net good' . . . The assumption is bolstered by the fear that if *this* method were not available, no moral reasoning would be possible. The fear is quite groundless; the intermediate principles of practical reasoning, which I call the requirements of practical reasonableness, disqualify many potential answers to moral problems. In some situations they indeed disqualify

[7] Richard A. McCormick, 'Ambiguity in Moral Choice' [1973] in McCormick and Paul Ramsey (eds.), *Doing Evil to Achieve Good* (Loyola UP, Chicago: 1978), at p. 38.

all possible choices save one; but ethics is not impotent in its bearing on the many situations in which there is no such uniquely correct answer to be identified. To treat the objective of ethics as the identification of uniquely correct answers is, as I said, a dogmatic legalism. Perhaps that is another residue of a deformed Christianity. Or perhaps it is an illegitimate extrapolation from the *procedural* requirement imposed on judges at law: that they must give judgment on every issue disputed between parties to litigation, and that judgment must be for one party rather than the other on every such issue.

IV.4 *Standard techniques of rationalization*

The basic human goods at stake in any morally significant situation of choice are incommensurable. This has the following consequence: all proportionalist arguments about what is morally required or morally permissible are, on all occasions, mere rationalization of conclusions arrived at on non-proportionalist grounds. Sometimes, of course, the rationalization may be helpful; that is, it may happen to bring to light some aspect of the situation which is morally relevant and which you might otherwise have overlooked. But never will a proportionalist argument do what it purports to do.

'Rationalization' is a pejorative word. But I do not use it for cheap rhetorical advantage, or as a term of personal abuse. Its use follows directly from my strictly philosophical thesis that, to arguments about morally significant problems, no practical conclusions *can* be justified, even in principle, by any appeal to overall or total consequences. For the corollary of this thesis is that all conclusions that purport to be so justified *must* have been arrived at for other reasons (if any).

Notice: I do not say that we should shun proportionalist argument for fear of distorting it by rationalization. My argument that proportionalist moral argument is senseless in no way depends on the risks of such distortion. Indeed, my argument tells against the view that there can be *distortion*; for only the properly shaped can be distorted, and my argument is that no proportionalist assessment could be properly shaped.

Proportionalist rationalizations are available, in relation to each moral problem, for any option that has any plausibility in view of the genuine requirements of practical reasonableness or in view of social conventions or sectarian desires or individual motivations. Once a moralist accepts proportionalist method, even as one methodological principle amonst others, he can produce arguments in favour of any solution which he already favours. All such arguments will be illegitimate, i.e. mere rationalizations. Moreover, to the extent that he seeks to deny his proportionalist method the exclusive status which it has in the classic utilitarian and other consequentalist systems, he can find no grounds for so restricting it which are not either (a) rationalizations or (b) grounds for excluding proportionalist method altogether.

The contemporary literature of proportionalism is rich with diverting rationalizations, whether by out-and-out direct ('act') utilitarians such as J. J. C. Smart and, *mutatis mutandis*, R. M. Hare and Timothy O'Connell, or by those theological proportionalists (such as Bruno Schüller and Richard McCormick) who hope to restrict their new-found method to cases considered 'hard' in progressive ecclesial circles and to solutions there favoured, today. I shall review some of the rationalizations adduced by these writers in relation to the very cases where proportionalist method *seems* able to commensurate: where there *seems* to be only one basic good at stake, and there seems to be sufficient reason to sacrifice one human life (or more than one) to save more lives.

Here, then, we approach explicitly the first of the three great questions of ethics (see I.3 above): Caiaphas's question 'Is it not better that one innocent person be put to death than that the whole people perish?' Nowadays, philosophers discuss this by way of a parable or thought-experiment: a sheriff foresees with practical certainty a riot in which many will be killed; but he also foresees that it can be avoided if he publicly hangs one innocent man.

A first, and most common, proportionalist rationalization is to suggest that such situations are so rare that they need not affect our judgment on the place of proportionalism in ethics.[8] With accomplished smoothness, many proportionalist

[8] See, e.g., J. J. C. Smart in Smart and Williams (eds.), *Utilitarianism: For and*

philosophers and theologians pass silently by some salient events of modern history: the adoption, first by the German, then the British and then the American governments and peoples, of the policy of deliberately destroying civilians in order to demoralize the enemy (to bring him to surrender unconditionally); and the adoption, by the British legislature and then by the American courts, of the policy of deliberately destroying unborn children in order to avoid the grave inconveniences that unwanted children visit on their parents and their community, a policy now expanding rapidly into the manner of dealing with the new-born. These are not mere fringe phenomena. Each has become a foundation of daily life. The policy of nuclear deterrence is the foundation of politics in the wealthy and relatively demilitarized democracies of the West; and the availability of termination of pregnancy is a fundament of the life-style and self-understanding of the generation which grew up with the deterrent. Why, then, should there be hesitation about the duty of the sheriff? How can the innocence of the one he must frame and 'execute' be decisive there, when it is not decisive for the decision to destroy a hundred thousand civilian men, women and children in a single night?

A second rationalization, still overlooking the moral phenomena I have just mentioned, declares that in the sheriff's case 'the entire institution of criminal law is at stake'.[9] 'Just think what would be the consequences of a moral education which contained no prohibition on murder!', says Hare about hard cases of this sort, and just think what would be the consequences of a legal system with no such prohibition.[10] The sophism here is evident enough. The question is whether moral education and the legal system should contain a rule about murder which is qualified by a clause allowing deliberate killing in cases of 'necessity', i.e. in cases where one genuinely and 'reasonably' believes that the bad consequences of not killing would be disproportionately

Against (CUP: 1973), pp. 70-1, 72; R. M. Hare, *Moral Thinking* (OUP, Oxford: 1981), 48, 132-5, 164.

[9] Bruno Schüller, 'The Double Effect in Catholic Thought: a Reevaluation', in McCormick and Ramsey, *Doing Evil to Achieve Good*, p. 177; Richard McCormick, *How Brave a New World?* (SCM, London: 1981), p. 428.
[10] Hare, op. cit., p. 133; also p. 135.

bad. After all, such a law has been on offer for decades in the Model Penal Code, whose draftsman Herbert Wechsler has lucidly explained its proportionalist (utilitarian) rationale;[11] and the principle of necessity as a complete and independent defence to a charge of homicide makes progress amongst lawyers and in the courts in many countries.

Let us test a little further the claim that 'the entire institution of the criminal law is at stake in the sheriff's decision'. Bruno Schüller, who made this claim, argued for it only by saying that the sheriff's act would be justified only if this conclusion, raised to a universally acknowledged and practical rule, would actually promote the common good, which is highly doubtful. But this argument obviously fails. No doubt everyone must be prepared to generalize or universalize the proposal he adopts, the choice he makes. But here the sheriff could say:

> My choice is to frame and kill the innocent man on one or other of the following two independently sufficient grounds: (i) that his innocence can probably be kept secret (so that my action will not encourage future lynch mobs to make similar demands);

I interrupt here to note that Hare imagines that this is the only ground available to the sheriff, and then rationalizes to the effect that keeping the secret is virtually impossible.[12] He overlooks the fact that the criminal law is an institution with resources for defending itself, resources the sheriff can rely on for his second ground:

> (ii) that there is a reasonable likelihood that the leaders of this mob can soon themselves be caught and punished in exemplary fashion for their incitement to murderous riot. And on either or both of these grounds, my action, when 'raised to a rule incorporating those alternative conditions as to secrecy or future punishment, and universally acknowledged and practised' by sheriffs, is clearly, or at least probably, for the common good.

[11] See American Law Institute, *Model Penal Code* (Philadelphia: 1980), arts. 2 and 3 (especially art. 3, headed 'Justification and Choice of Evils'); and commentary in *Tentative Draft No. 8* (Philadelphia: 1958), pp. 5-10; and H. Wechsler and J. Michael, 'A Rationale of the Law of Homicide' (1937) 37 *Columbia Law Review*, 701 at 738-9. [12] Hare, *Moral Thinking*, pp. 48, 164.

That is a quite sufficient answer both to Schüller's argument and to the argument launched by Richard McCormick in 1973 that the sheriff's surrender to the mob's demands would 'encourage[] a type of injustice which in the long run would render many more lives vulnerable'.[13]

Indeed, in 1978 McCormick abandoned that argument and indicated his dissatisfaction with Schüller's argument, while at the same time defending Schüller's claim itself, viz., that the sheriff's act is unjustified because somehow the whole institution of the criminal law is at stake. In a moment I shall examine McCormick's new rationalization, which announces a new and remarkable form of proportionalism. But first, I shall look at something else the sheriff might say about arguments based on 'the long run'.

The sheriff might point out that, according to the leading contemporary philosophical proponent of utilitarianism, J. J. C. Smart, all utilitarian or consequentialist ethical systems are 'fatally affected' if they are not allowed the unproven but 'plausible enough' postulate that 'remote consequences' can be left out of account. Such long-run consequences are like ripples in the pond; they die away.[14] Well, as a matter of fact, Smart concedes that they do not get any less;[15] so he then leaps to the postulate that they over the long run 'cancel one another out'.[16] Here we see rationalization in full flight. For if good and bad 'remote consequences' cancel one another out, then they surely will also 'cancel out' the good or bad immediate consequences; if about a million good remote consequences cancel out about a million bad remote consequences, then those two million will certainly cancel out the two or three good (or bad) consequences which I had in mind when I chose to do my act. Of course, in real life we do reason as if we accepted the 'ripple in the pond' postulate. But that is because in real life we do not accept the proportionalist postulate that each of us is *responsible for* 'total' or 'overall' consequences, or for maximizing total or overall net good, or anything like that. The 'ripple in the pond' postulate can be defended, not on an

---

[13] McCormick, in McCormick and Ramsey, *Doing Evil*, p. 33.
[14] Smart, 'An outline of a system of utilitarian ethics', in J. J. C. Smart and Bernard Willams, *Utilitarianism: for and against*, p. 34.
[15] Ibid., p. 34.   [16] Ibid., pp. 38, 65.

analysis of actual causal influences, but only on the basis of a theory of responsibility (i.e. a theory of practical reasonableness) which proportionalism radically rejects. So our sheriff may well say:

> If I don't hang this one man, I'm sure that a score or more of innocents are going to die nastily. As for the longer-run consequences, you proportionalists yourselves say they cancel each other out or for some other (unclear) reason can be ignored. So why all these appeals from the known to the unknown?

Among those who published consequentialist reasonings about the sheriff case, early in its career as a philosophical test-case, was Alan Donagan. He argued for an exception to the rule against murder and framing, to allow the sheriff's action: the case would be rare, it need never become known that the victim was framed, and '(as the Dreyfus case showed), many people are comforted rather than appalled by the thought that their officials act on Caiaphas's principle ...'[17] Another proportionalist replied, rehearsing the arguments still being used today by Hare, Schüller and others. Donagan tells us how this finally opened his own eyes; for as he worked on his rejoinder, 'our joint performance began to appear comic ... we were debating, not exchanging scientific results ... On this debated issue, no utilitarian calculations are available, mistaken or otherwise: there is nothing but advocacy.'[18]

IV.5 A new form of rationalization

Like Alan Donagan, Richard McCormick has realized that the sheriff case cannot reasonably be settled by appeals to long-run consequences. McCormick, indeed, has conceded (since about 1978), that the incommensurability of basic goods means that it is impossible to identify an objective 'overall lesser evil' alternative to an 'overall greater evil'. But, unlike Donagan, he wishes to retain a proportionalist ethical method.

---

[17] Alan Donagan, *The Theory of Morality* (University of Chicago P., Chicago and London: 1977), p. 204, summarising his 'Is There a Credible Form of Utilitarianism?', Michael D. Bayles (ed.), *Contemporary Utilitarianism* (Doubleday, New York: 1958), pp. 193-5.
[18] Donagan, *The Theory of Morality*, p. 204.

His new technique of rationalizing is not familiar in secular philosophical circles, but it is widely shared in certain theological circles and repays study. We can trace it through McCormick's recent discussions both of the thought-experiment of the sheriff (whom he calls, sometimes, a 'judge'), and of countervalue nuclear strategy (i.e. the deliberate destruction of civilians to demoralize the enemy: e.g. 'terror bombing').

First, then, McCormick's new analysis of the sheriff case: the conclusion of the analysis is that 'what appears to be a lifesaving action by the [sheriff] is really at odds with the very value of life—is disproportionate'.[19] And the reason McCormick gives is this:

extortion by definition accepts the necessity of doing non-moral evil to get others to cease their wrongdoing. The acceptance of such a necessity is an implied denial of human freedom. But since human freedom is a basic value associated with other basic values (in this case, life), undermining it *also thereby undermines life*. In sum, extortion, as life undermining, is not *materia apta* (Janssens), is disproportionate.[20]

(Notice that the extortion referred to is not, as you might expect and as McCormick himself had in mind in 1973, the lynch mob's extortion of the life of an innocent. Rather, according to McCormick in 1978, the extortion is practised *by the sheriff* against the mob to get them to desist from murderous riot.)

The new analysis thus makes three important claims: (i) about denial of freedom; (ii) that denial of freedom undermines life; and (iii) about proportionality. The relation between the second and third of these claims becomes clearer in a parallel passage:

because of the association of basic goods, an assault on one (liberty) will bring harm to another (life) and . . . therefore judicial murder is *in itself* a disproportionate means. It is not *materia apta* to the goal (preservation of life) because it denies in the means the very value sought in the end.[21]

That gives the essence of the new theological version of proportionalism. The ambition is evidently to avoid reliance

[19] *Doing Evil*, p. 260.   [20] Ibid.   [21] Ibid., p. 250.

on the absurd calculus of long-term consequences; for the passage just quoted continues:

In doing so, it will certainly have long-range consequences, but it is not them that constitute the disproportion: they help to reveal it. Thus the term consequences, as I would read it, refers to the present support of or undermining of the value being sought, a support or undermining that occurs through association with other goods.[22]

But it is not so easy to transform proportionalism from the inside. The plain fact is that McCormick's new key concept— that denial of one basic value undermines the basic value being sought in the action—is a concept entirely dependent for its intelligibility on the (speculatively supposed) *long run*. This is disguised, in the passage just quoted, by the phrase 'present support of or undermining of . . .' But in a parallel passage published in the same year McCormick reveals his continued reliance upon traditional proportionalist methods:

One who unjustifiably takes human life also undermines other human goods, and these human goods, once weakened or undermined will affect the very good of life itself.[23]

Already, we notice, the schema is 'once X, Y will . . .' And in the case of the sheriff

the manner of protecting the good (human life—by framing one inno-cent person) will undermine it *in the long run* by serious injury to an associated good (human liberty) . . .[24]

Thus we see McCormick (and with him many another theo-logian) hovering uncertainly between two radically distinct conceptions of proportionality: (A) an act is proportionate if and only if present good aspects and immediate consequences, when weighed against long-run bad consequences, outweigh those long-run consequences; (B) an act is proportionate if and only if, in the present act itself, the means selected are themselves, here and now, apt to the chosen end itself (as distinct from further consequences).

To make conception (B) intelligible, and usable for his purposes, McCormick (talking of undermining 'associated

---

[22] Ibid.
[23] Richard A. McCormick, *Notes on Moral Theology 1965 through 1980* (University Press of America, Washington, DC: 1981), p. 719 [1978].
[24] Ibid., p. 720 [1978].

goods') appeals to the long-term effects of those means. The efforts to differentiate the new conception of proportionality thus contradict the very rationale of those efforts, which was to get away from straightforward consequentialist reliance on long-term consequences. But the efforts are real enough; they lead McCormick to make the remarkable claim that 'bad consequences occur because the act was *in itself disproportionate*'[25]—as if his whole discussion were not about 'conflict situations' or 'tragic circumstances' in which the aftermath of *any* choice (or failure to choose) seems certain to include some very bad consequences!

Still, the new conception is worth exploring further. Let us hear McCormick stating it one more time:

The phrase 'proportionate reason' is not convertible with the notion of 'better results' or 'net good'. Rather it means that the value being sought will not be undermined by the contemplated action. *Proportionate* in the usage 'proportionate reason' refers to a relationship to the basic good in question. Thus where there is a question of taking life, such taking is proportionate only if it is, all things considered, the better service of *life itself* in the tragic circumstances.[26]

In the words of Louis Janssens, adopted by McCormick, 'the principle which has been affirmed in the end must not be negated by the means'; there is to be no 'intrinsic contradiction between the means and the end'.[27]

But suppose the value I am seeking is truth, to be attained through scientific research and experiments which involve directly killing human beings. How is truth 'negated' or 'contradicted' by such killing? The new theory seems to have no critique of fanaticism, which selects one basic value and subordinates some or all other basic values to the rank of means, and does so with, perhaps, practical intelligence and 'prudence'.

But now suppose (*per impossibile*, I believe) that the new proportionalists developed some such critique of fanaticism, and that they also managed to show, somehow, that experimental killings would, somehow, in the long run, 'undermine'

[25] McCormick, in *Doing Evil*, p. 261; also pp. 234-5 [1977].

[26] McCormick, in *Doing Evil*, p. 201 [1977].

[27] Janssens, 'Ontic Evil and Moral Evil' (1972) 4 *Louvain Studies* 115 at p. 142, quoted by McCormick in *Doing Evil*, p. 202.

or 'negate' scientific research and the cause of truth. Then we would be confronted by a more fundamental weakness of the new theory: the theory looks away from the real moral evil, the real violation of right or of rights, towards an artificially constructed evil. In reality, the fanatical scientist's wrongful deed is murder, and the person wronged is his victim. But the new theorists say that the wrong done is, formally, self-contradiction and, materially, research-undermining and damage to truth; the implication is that the persons wronged are future scientists, future generations who might have benefited from science, and so on—anyone rather than the victim killed under our noses.

Test this now in the case—not, alas, a mere thought-experiment—of terror bombing of civilians. Here is McCormick's 1978 account; it parallels his account of the sheriff thought-experiment:

Making innocent (noncombatant) persons the object of our targeting is a form of extortion in international affairs that contains an implicit denial of human freedom. Human freedom is undermined when extortionary actions are accepted and elevated and universalised. Because such freedom is an associated good upon which the very good of life heavily depends, undermining it in the manner of my defence of life is undermining life itself—is disproportionate.[28]

So, just as the lynch mob 'can cease their evil-doing without our doing harm to make them cease', and 'to yield to their demand would be a denial to them of their own freedom', so too,

if a nation is wrongfully aggressive . . . that nation can and must cease and desist from wrongful aggression without our harming innocents to make that nation do so. There is no *necessary connection* between our doing harm to noncombatants . . . and that nation's ceasing unjust aggression. To say that there is would be to insult the humanity of the aggressor by denying his liberty.[29]

Thus the new proportionalists identify two evils in terror bombing. First, the evil of threatening future generations by undermining life *by undermining or denying freedom here and now*—an altogether mysterious process of speculative 'association of goods', a process which McCormick says he

---

[28] McCormick in *Doing Evil*, p. 236 [1977]; verbatim in *Notes on Moral Theology*, p. 720 [1978].   [29] McCormick in *Doing Evil*, p. 237 [1977].

knows 'spontaneously, non-discursively and therefore ob-
scurely to a large extent . . .' by his 'emotions and religious
commitments' and by 'instinct'.[30] And secondly, there is the
evil of insulting the humanity . . . *of the aggressor*.

Thus, in the new proportionalists' analysis, the direct
insult to the humanity *of the innocents directly killed* disappears from—or never gets into—the moral focus. Test their
analysis with a more homely example: a mugger threatens me
with death unless I give him $5. I hand him the $5. The new
proportionalists will say, presumably, that I have insulted the
mugger's humanity by denying his freedom; for (like the
lynch mob and the aggressor nation) he could and should
have chosen, at any point, to cease and desist from his
mugging. Presumably, on this story, by denying his freedom
I have undermined the 'associated good' of life which so
'heavily depends' on freedom. So *I* am morally responsible
for numberless killings in the future . . .!

The new proportionalists have no monopoly on implausible
and misdirected identifications of the evil and wrong in plain
murder. (Note: by 'murder' I mean directly killing the innocent; I do not define murder as wrongful killing, even though
I hold that murder is a killing which is always wrongful.)
Utilitarians and consequentialists of more conventional type
have always been obliged by their method either to favour
plain murder in certain cases or to produce rationalizations
which, apart from their implausibility, *look in the wrong
direction*.

R. M. Hare, for example, is now saying that what was
wrong with the tortures laid on to entertain the Roman
populace at the arena was that there were other ways in
which they could have got their pleasures:

The right thing to have done from the utilitarian point of view would
have been to have chariot races or football games or other less atrocious
sports; modern experience shows that they can generate just as much
excitement.[31]

Hare concludes that a wise utilitarian would therefore try to
educate children to acquire the 'intuition' that such tortures

---

[30] Ibid., p. 250; also pp. 251, 227.
[31] R. M. Hare, *Moral Thinking*, p. 142.

are wrong (though for a critical thinker, he says, they are only prima facie wrong).

This, of course, is mere rationalization. 'Modern experience' has not shown that football is as exciting as human bloodsports; there has been no experiment in comparison. But worse: the whole argument fails to identify the real wrong done to the victims of fun-killings and entertaining tortures. The wrongfulness of such practices does not depend on the question whether those watching get sufficiently or insufficiently exquisite satisfactions from these compared with other entertainments. When homicides are painless, utilitarians have always found themselves obliged to say that the wrong consists in the apprehension caused to the survivors who henceforth have to worry about being killed off privily. Once more, they mislocate both the harm and the wrong. The person really harmed and wronged is, of course, the victim, not the survivors. But of that wrong, proportionalism new or old has no coherent account.

Any moral theory which admits into its method even a purportedly restricted proportionalist principle is going to overlook the wrong in certain serious wrongs. If those practices are admitted by such theories to be wrongful, the wrongfulness will be misidentified and mislocated. It will be alleged to consist in considerations not only unconvincing in their causal hypotheses but also intrinsically beside-the-point in their identification of the person harmed and of the nature of the harm, and thus of the person *wronged*.

In the next chapter, I discuss more adequate accounts of why it is wrong to do the sorts of things we have seen both condemned and defended by proportionalist rationalization. I move a step closer to answering Caiaphas's question (IV.4). I begin that discussion, however, by offering a still more basic critique of proportionalist theories, a critique that centres on the second of the three great questions (I.3): 'Is it better to do wrong or to suffer it?' And I defend non-proportionalist theory against the claim that any moral condemnation of, say, all direct killing of the innocent *must* be based on a covert, unadmitted proportionalism.

NOTES

IV.1

William James, Bertrand Russell, Roscoe Pound, and utilitarian pragmatism . . . See *Natural Law and Natural Rights*, pp. 132, 293; R. S. Summers, 'Pragmatic Instrumentalism in Twentieth Century American Legal Thought' (1981) 66 *Cornell Law Rev.* 861 at 875-7.

Preference utilitarianism . . . R. M. Hare's exposition of his preference utilitarianism, in his *Moral Thinking* (1981), clearly exposes many of its problems. The concept of preference is introduced under the aegis of rational choice (and 'to have a preference is to accept a prescription': p. 91), but the only preferences that get counted are the preferences (of the chooser and of 'others', i.e. sentient animals, called 'people' 'for brevity's sake': pp. 90-1) 'with regard to experiences which the preferer is currently having' (either now or in some future state of affairs now under his/its consideration) (p. 104). Of preferences concerning states of affairs which the chooser will not experience (vicariously or otherwise), Hare says 'I am inclined to think that we ought [to count these], but that I cannot at present do so' (p. 104). The (further?) 'simplifying assumption' is made that no preference is to count unless its satisfaction is logically and factually consistent with having 'a dominant or overriding preference now that the satisfaction of our now-for-now and then-for-then [i.e. current experience] preferences should be maximized' (p. 105). After these drastic and confessedly arbitrary restrictions have been made, Hare is inclined to call his theory a 'happiness' rather than a 'preference' utilitarianism (p. 103).

'Mixed [or moderate] teleology' . . . See, e.g., McCormick, *Notes on Moral Theology*, pp. 650 [1977], 762 [1979]. Contrast Bruno Schüller, 'The Double effect in Catholic Thought: a Reevaluation', in McCormick and Ramsey, *Doing Evil to Achieve Good*, at pp. 167-8.

'Proportionalism' . . . For a survey (and a critique on rather different lines from mine), see Servais Pinckaers, 'La question des actes intrinsèquement mauvais et le "proportionnalisme"' (1982) *Revue Thomiste*, 181-212.

Not all references to 'for a proportionate reason' are proportionalist . . . For example: the English translation of the Sacred Congregation for the Doctrine of the Faith's *Declaration on Euthanasia* dated 5 May 1980 makes three references to proportion. (i) Medical experts can judge when the pain and suffering imposed on a patient by certain techniques are 'out of proportion with the benefits which he or she may gain from such techniques' [graviora quam utilitates quae inde ei afferri possunt]; as the reference to *medical* expertise makes clear, this judgment about disproportion pertains to points on a single scale, i.e. the scale of pain and suffering: the matters on each side of the comparison are restricted to *pain and suffering* and *relief from pain and suffering*. No commensurating of the incommensurable is proposed.

(ii) Medical experts may also judge that 'the investment in instruments and personnel is disproportionate to the results foreseen' [non respondet effectibus qui praevidentur]; this should be regarded as an invitation to the *medical* expert (whose judgment is being discussed at this point in the Declaration) to consider the proposed 'investment in instruments and personnel' in the light not of an open-ended calculus of all the good effects of keeping this patient alive (which would involve a senseless weighing of incommensurables), but rather of his normal system of priorities—a system which is established not by calculus but by commitment. (See further *Natural Law and Natural Rights*, pp. 111, 117–18, 132.) (iii) Refusal to undergo risky or burdensome treatment is not the equivalent of suicide, but rather may be 'a wish to avoid the application of a medical procedure disproportionate to the results that can be expected' [cura vitandi laboriosum medicae artis apparatum cui par sperandorum effectuum utilitas non respondeat]; this, too, should be taken as a reference, not to a calculation of moral obligation by weighing the incommensurable goods of longer life and freedom from pain, but to a person's choice (not unrestrained by consideration of his existing moral responsibilities, e.g. to his family), a choice by which that patient establishes for himself what counts (for him) as *par utilitas* (literally: equivalent benefit) in these respects. See further *Euthanasia and Clinical Practice: Trends, Principles and Alternatives* (Linacre Centre, London: 1982), pp. 29-30, 46-9, 53.

IV.2

Computation of the overall 'balance of good and evil' (flowing from morally significant choices) is impossible . . . For an example of the attempt to do the impossible, see G. E. M. Anscombe's undergraduate pamphlet, 'The Justice of the Present War Examined' [1939], in her *Collected Philosophical Papers*, vol. III, at pp. 79-81.

Utilitarian or consequentialist ethical method is open to objections other than for its impracticability or senselessness . . . See Donagan, *The Theory of Morality*, pp. 200-1.

'The totality of what will happen if one decides in a certain way' . . . On Prior's proof that this concept is senseless unless determinism is true, see also P. T. Geach, *The Virtues* (CUP, Cambridge: 1977), p. 99; *Providence and Evil* (CUP, Cambridge: 1977), p. 82. The utilitarian could give some sense to his method by revising it to speak of *objectively* probable total consequences (see Prior, *Time and Tense*, p. 53). But there is no theory of objective probabilities, as honest proponents of utilitarian method admit: see, e.g., J. J. C. Smart, in Smart and Williams, *Utilitarianism: for and against*, pp. 40-1. See also Donagan, *The Theory of Morality*, p. 200.

'Choose the lesser evil' . . . For the very restricted range of this maxim, properly interpreted, see Donagan, *The Theory of Morality*, pp. 152, 155; Roberti (ed.), *Dictionary of Moral Theology* (Burns and Oates,

London: 1962), pp. 705-6; Grisez, 'The Moral Implications of a Nuclear Deterrent' (1982) 2 *Center Journal* 1 at 18n.

IV.5

'Avoid self-contradiction' as the master principle of the new proportionalism . . . For the earliest and clearest formulation, see Peter Knauer, 'La détermination du bien et du mal moral par le principe du double effet' (1965) 87 *Nouvelle Revue Théologique*, 365-76 at pp. 368-71; Knauer, 'The Hermeneutic Function of the Principle of Double Effect' (1967) 12 *Natural Law Forum*, 132-62, reprinted in Charles E. Curran and Richard A. McCormick, *Readings in Moral Theology No. 1: Moral Norms and Catholic Tradition* (Paulist Press, New York: 1979), pp. 1-39 at p. 13: 'immoral acts are in the last analysis self-contradictions . . . there is a long-run contradiction in reality between the value sought and the way of achieving it'. Knauer's argumentation makes clear that his reason for this quasi-Kantian interpretation of proportionalism is his awareness of the incommensurability of basic goods: see pp. 11-12.

One who regards murder as always wrong need not define 'murder' as 'wrongful killing' . . . See *Euthanasia and Clinical Practice*, p. 24.

The victim of a painless murder is harmed . . . See Joel Feinberg, 'Harm and Self-interest', in Hacker and Raz (eds.), *Law, Morality and Society* (Clarendon Press, Oxford: 1977) at pp. 299-308.

V
'Kantian Principles' and Ethics

V.1 *Proportionalism and the Pauline principle*

'Do not choose directly against any basic human good': that is an intermediate principle (III.4) which, in the tradition of ethical reflection and teaching, we find expressed, or approached, in at least three famous formulations.

The formulation first in time is also the most generic; it asserts the priority not only of that intermediate principle but of all the other principles of practical reasonableness (e.g. the principle against unfairness). It has been called the Democritean principle, because formulated by Democritus of Abdera in fifth-century Athens. But I shall call it Socrates' principle; for Plato tells us that Socrates not only taught it but also lived by it, and it was his expression of it that really secured its place in the tradition: 'It is better to suffer wrong than to do it'. We shall see (V.2) that proportionalism makes nonsense of Socrates' principle.

But it will be helpful to begin by attending to the less radical principle, which can be called Pauline since it is implied, and virtually formulated, in Paul's letter to the Romans (*Romans* 3: 8; also 6: 1, 15): 'Evil may not be done for the sake of good'. My discussion of the Pauline and Socratic principles will conclude the main part of my critique of proportionalism.

I then consider why my formulation of the principle against attacking basic human goods should be preferred to Kant's similar categorical imperative: 'Do not ever treat humanity, whether in your own person or in another's, merely as a means'.

The point at stake in all these formulations has, of course, a more popular, common-sense formulation: 'The end does not justify the means'. For use in disciplined critical thinking, however, that saying needs reformulation. For all justified means are justified precisely by their end(s). Sometimes, perhaps, no more is meant than: '*This* means is not justified by *this* end'. More often however, there is an implicit appeal to principle: 'There are some acts which cannot be justified by any end'. This, then, directly challenges proportionalism in all its forms. In the previous chapter I started to consider why that challenge is justified.

The early Christian theologians reflected on this matter. In St John's Gospel, in which no word is casually uttered, we find Caiaphas's question not once but twice, in widely separated passages (*John* 11: 50; 18: 14): 'Is it not better that one innocent person be put to death than that the whole people perish?' The question is raised generically, not just about that particular 'one innocent'. But since that particular person's fate hangs on the answer, the question by its general formulation and its particular context appeals to, clarifies and powerfully reinforces the faithful reader's acknowledgment of the principle embodied in the answer 'No!' (In the language of a later theology, 'revelation' is here being offered as 'confirming and illuminating the natural law'.)

St Paul had to confront the issue of principle polemically. For in the first ferment of belief in man's definitive redemption by God, some believers opined that wrongdoing (sin) is tolerable or even desirable because it affords occasion for God to accomplish His redemptive work; and the more sin the better, for thus the more opportunity for the giving and receiving of grace: see *Romans* 6: 1, 15 and context. And some people claimed that Paul's own teaching carried the same message: human unfaithfulness, unholiness, untruthfulness give God glory by prompting Him to demonstrate His fidelity, holiness, and truthfulness; so my lies and infidelities bring about good states of affairs and should not be judged sins at all.

All this Paul vigorously repudiates. It would, he says, 'be the same as saying: *Do evil as a means to good*. Some slanderers have accused us of teaching this, but they are justly condemned': *Romans* 3: 8.

In his repudiations of the heretical sophism, St Paul hints at the reason why no clear-headed Jew or Christian can be a proportionalist (consequentialist, utilitarian . . .). For fundamental to these faiths is a notion of God's providence: that out of every evil, including moral evil (sin),

God will bring the good that He intends for the whole
universe of times, places, persons . . . Now proportionalism in
all its forms proposes that we guide our choices by seeking
what promises an overall greater good and lesser evil, 'on the
whole and in the long run . . .' And when combined with
belief in providence, that proposal yields the following
ethical method:

> If in doubt about what to do, *do anything*. Whatever
> deed one does, one can be certain that on the whole and
> in the long run it will have been for the best; and thus, if
> the deed one does is what one chose to do, one can be
> certain that that choice was right.

This conclusion, of course, contradicts the fundamental
Judaeo-Christian affirmation that one can choose, open-
eyed, between right and wrong, and choose wrong: deliberate
sin is possible. Proportionalist explanations of 'right' and
'wrong' are thus not rationally open to Jews or Christians.
    The foregoing argument needs no expansion. But if we
reflect on it, we can see that the collision between proportionalism and Christianity has its origins in the proportionalist's implicit proposal to undertake the very responsibility
that Christianity, like Judaism, ascribes to God Himself: of
securing the overall greater good or lesser evil, on the whole
and taking into account the long run. In the next section,
quite apart from Judaeo-Christian beliefs, I shall show how
the proportionalist's imaginary perspective, as a God-like
figure surveying possible worlds and choosing the world
that embodies greater good or lesser evil, is a perspective that
is simply not open to human practical reason.
    Let me return for a moment, however, to the principle
implicitly taught by Paul: 'Do not do evil, even for the
sake of good'. Proportionalists, if they are Christian theologians, are bound to attribute some meaning to Paul's
principle. But their efforts to do so yield only gibberish:
'Do not, [even] for the sake of proportionate reason, do
anything that does not have proportionate reason'. (In consequentialist terminology: 'Do not, [even] for the sake of
overall best [or better] consequences, do anything that does
not have overall best consequences'.) Understandably, therefore, the proportionalist theologians prefer to set Paul's

principle aside, as empty. They teach that 'evil may be done, but only for the sake of greater good'. I have said much, and will say more, about the muddles involved in this proposal. Let me here make one point about terminology.

In common speech, as used in translating Paul's saying, 'doing evil' invariably means 'doing moral evil', i.e. wrong-doing: choosing an *act* that should not be chosen, making a *choice* that should not be made. Thus when the proportion-alist says that 'evil may sometimes be done . . .', he uses the phrase 'doing evil' in a radically different sense; for he does not *mean* that doing wrong is sometimes the right thing to do. He intends to be talking about the so-called 'pre-moral evil' brought about by choices, which can be 'outweighed' by the 'pre-moral goods' they are supposed to bring about. But often we find the proportionalist overlooking the termino-logical consequences of his shift of attention from choices to outcomes; he has disguised the shift, even from himself, by retaining the phrase 'doing evil', and related phrases such as 'evil act' or 'imperfect act'. Richard McCormick, for example, says that 'everyone admits' that a life-saving amputation 'is an imperfect act'.[1] In reality, however, no one save those con-fused by bad philosophy admits any such thing; we do not con-fuse the quality of the surgeon's *act* with the imperfect (though reasonably desired) resulting state or condition of the amputee. Loss of one's leg is a bad thing, an evil; lack of a leg is an imperfection. But the life-saving acts of amputation are not imperfect; they are not *doing evil*, not at all, not even a little bit . . . Common speech thus, without confusion, makes a distinction which proportionalism proposes to eliminate.

I now turn to examine the deep misconceptions of practical reasoning that underlie that proposal. These misconceptions come to light when one considers why proportionalism makes nonsense of Socrates' principle: 'It is better to suffer wrong than to do it'.

V.2   *Proportionalism and Socrates' principle*

It will be helpful to have in mind Socrates' own story (accord-ing to Plato) of a choice to suffer wrong rather than do it:

The Thirty Commissioners summoned me and four others to the Round

---

[1] McCormick, *Notes on Moral Theology*, p. 631 [1977].

Chamber and ordered us to go and fetch Leon of Salamis from his home for liquidation . . . their object being to implicate as many people as possible in their evil . . . When we came out of the Round Chamber the other four went off to Salamis and arrested Leon, and I went home.[2]

Had the tyranny of the Thirty Commissioners not collapsed soon afterwards, Socrates' refusal to help liquidate Leon would have earned him the same sort of wrong: death at the hands of political gangsters. He had every reason to anticipate that; his choice was indeed 'to suffer wrong rather than do it'.

Socrates' principle that such a choice is better than the choice to do wrong is fundamental to the system of ideas we call ethics or morality. To explicate it is the task Plato set himself in the *Republic*, and Aristotle treats it as an obvious and fundamental implication of the ideas of justice and of right and wrong (virtue and vice, practical reasonableness . . .).[3] The Second Vatican Council formally teaches that such offences against the human person as murder, abortion, deliberate suicide, slave-trading, and so on, 'degrade [*inquinant*] those who so act more than those who suffer the wrong'.[4]

But how can this be so? We will not find this principle intelligible if we interpret it as making a comparative evaluation of states of affairs, or outcomes of choice.

The most radical difference between proportionalist and non-proportionalist ethics is that the proportionalist locates his criterion of right choice exclusively in the expected *outcomes* of alternative choices, i.e. in the states of affairs resulting from the choice. As I noted in discussing consequentialism (IV.1), some proportionalists wish to include in their assessment an evaluation of the action (i.e. chosen behaviour) itself, as well as of its consequences. But their evaluation of that action is as one more state of affairs, or one more event, among the other states of affairs or events which together constitute the outcome of a choice. The proportionalist seeks to include the acting subject within the horizon of his own assessments and choices as one object

---

[2] Plato, *Apology* 32c–e.   [3] *Nic. Eth.* V, 11: 1138a28–b5.
[4] Pastoral Constitution on the Church in the Modern World, 1965 (*Gaudium et Spes*), 27.

amongst others, and to include his choice and his behaviour as one state of affairs or event amongst others. Anselm Müller has illuminated this 'eventistic' character of proportionalism by way of demonstrating that proportionalism makes nonsense of Socrates' principle.[5] I shall look first at his demonstration, and then at the wider implications of proportionalism's neglect of the first-person singular perspective (i.e. the transparency) of practical reasoning, deliberation and choice.

No eventistic ethics can accommodate (i.e. is compatible with) the Socratic principle. For any ethics that is eventistic will treat the following two formulations as equivalent:

(1) It is true of every person x that x should act on the principle that 'I ought not to do V'.

(2) It is true of every person x that x not doing V is a proportionately better state of affairs [event] than x doing V.

In specifying an event (x doing V) the occurrence of which is proportionately worse than its non-occurrence and which therefore ought not to occur, proposition (2) certainly seems at first glance to be equivalent to proposition (1), specifying a rule or principle of choice for x to follow, such that if he does follow it the proportionately less desirable event mentioned in (2) will indeed not occur. But the equivalence is quite illusory. The non-equivalence of (1) and (2) can be rigorously demonstrated in relation to at least one principle or rule of choice: the Socratic principle. Let us formulate it as Plato's Socrates himself did, i.e. not, primarily, as a comparison between states of affairs as better and worse, more and less harmful, but rather as a principle of choice: 'If it were necessary either to do wrong or to suffer it, I should choose to suffer rather than to do it.'[6]

Thus it is an instance of (1):

(1a) It is true of every person x that x should act on the principle that 'I ought to suffer wrong rather than do wrong'.

Now an eventistic ethic would have to translate that as:

(2a) It is true of every person x that x suffering wrong is a proportionately better state of affairs than x doing wrong.

---

[5] Anselm W. Müller, 'Radical Subjectivity: Morality versus Utilitarianism' (1977) 19 *Ratio* 115–32.   [6] *Gorgias* 469c.

But (2a) contains a hidden self-contradiction. For (2a) yields, for instance,

(2b) It is true of any persons x, y, z that x suffering wrong from y is a better state of affairs than x doing wrong to z.

And from (2b) there can be derived not only

(2c) a suffering wrong from b is a better state of affairs than a doing wrong to b

but also its opposite:

(2d) b suffering wrong from a is a better state of affairs than b doing wrong to a.

In other words, the rendering of Socrates' principle attempted by the eventist (viz., (2a)) entails that in a given situation one and the same state of affairs is both 'proportionately better' and 'proportionately worse', i.e. both more and less desirable (or valuable or choice-worthy). But such contradiction is as intolerable in ethics as in any other intelligent activity. So proportionalism, and all other forms of eventism, can find no place for Socrates' principle.

The eventist is likely to protest that everyone can subscribe to Socrates' principle because it is trivial: everyone agrees that it is always wrong to do wrong and worse to do so than to do anything that is not wrong; so Socrates cannot have intended to do more than deny that one may do *whatever* is necessary to avoid suffering wrong, a denial with which the eventist will agree (one may not kill a hundred to save one's own life). But this protest misses the point. Imagine that Socrates was first *invited* by the Thirty to murder the innocent Leon. Socrates will judge that wrong and refuse. So, too, will the eventist—at least, probably, and depending on the circumstances as he 'assesses' them. So now the Thirty threaten Socrates with death if he does not comply; and threaten the eventist, too, with death if *he* does not comply. Here the eventist must either:

(A) simply abandon the judgment that to kill Leon would be to wrong him, and re-do his moral reasoning to discover whether the killing of L by S is a proportionately better event than the killing of S by the Thirty; his

conclusion could be that killing L is the right thing, or
that undergoing death at the hands of the Thirty is the
right thing, or that there is no way of telling which
choice will have best consequences . . .

or

(B) retain his former judgment that killing Leon would be
wrong, but balance that against the new factor that to
choose not to wrong Leon would be to choose to undergo an equivalent wrong at the hand of the Thirty; so
that there is no way of identifying the overall better
choice . . .

The actual Socrates, on the other hand, confronts the threat
with the same judgment as before, that to kill Leon would
be a wrong (and wrong); and the Socratic principle affirms
that that first judgment remains decisive in the face of the
symmetrical wrong threatened by the Thirty. (Indeed, the
Socratic principle as used by Socrates goes further; it affirms
that the judgment that killing Leon would be wrong remains
decisive even though the result of choosing not to wrong
Leon will be two wrongs instead of one—since the Thirty are
going to wrong Leon *anyway*.) Thus one can say neither that
the Socratic principle is trivial nor that it means no more
than 'there are limits to the things you can do to avoid
suffering'.

The point, as Müller shows, is this. On any eventist analysis,
the state of affairs in which *a* wrongs *b* is symmetrical with
the state of affairs in which *b* wrongs *a*, and this symmetry
of equally bad states of affairs is not disturbed by the fact
that I am *a*. Morality, on the other hand, can accommodate
the Socratic maxim, because in my practical moral thinking
I cannot ignore the fact that one of two intrinsically bad
alternatives would be realized through me.

The Socratic maxim implicitly asserts that the 'direction'
of action is morally significant in at least two respects: (i)
intentional infliction of harm is not morally forbidden where
it is by way of just punishment or justified self-defence (see
V.5 below); but the harm-doing act must be *directed at the
wrongdoer or wrongful aggressor*, and it is not permissible to
intentionally harm an innocent bystander (say, Leon) in

order to persuade the wrongdoer (say, the Thirty) to desist from his present or threatened wrong. (ii) What matters to the person acting is the wrongfulness of *his* action; the fact that there may or will be an equivalent or greater wrong done by *someone else* cannot be morally decisive for the person now acting; Solzhenitsyn's Nobel prize speech takes up this theme:

There is one simple step a simple courageous man can take—not to take part in the lie, not to give his support to false actions. Let this principle [sc. the lie that masks the method of violence] enter the world and even dominate the world—*but not through me*.[7]

Here, then, we see another fundamental implication of the fact that ethics is the work of *practical* reason, of *my* seeking to determine what it is reasonable (good or right) for *me* to do—i.e., more simply but equivalently, my seeking to *determine what to do*. Proportionalism, as eventistic, treats ethical deliberation as fundamentally a 'speculative' assessment of the proportions of good and ill embodied in and resulting from states of affairs or events, including the state(s) of affairs or event(s) constituted by my choosing and my behaviour. A non-eventistic ethics, on the other hand, takes account of the fact that there is one person 'whose possible modes of behaviour I can present to my will not only in expressions of the form "*x* does so and so", but also in expressions of the form "to do so and so"'.[8] The deliberate behaviour of this (and only this) person can, and in general must, be the object of my intention (i.e. the subject-matter of my choice) in a way other than by my having the intention *that JMF does so-and-so (and I am JMF)*. Rather, my intention is primarily *to do so-and-so*.[9] (Note, again, the philosophical phenomenon of transparency: the 'I' (and any other reference to the subject) drops out of the statement of what it is I intend, just as, at the beginning of the present paragraph, the phrase 'it is reasonable for me' could be dropped from the characterization of practical reasoning.)

Proportionalism ignores the difference between these two formulations of intention. But the difference is confirmed, as

---

[7] Alexander Solzhenitsyn, *Nobel Prize Lecture* [1972], section 7 (trans. Nicholas Bethell, Stenvalley Press, London: 1973), p. 53.

[8] Müller, 'Radical Subjectivity . . .', p. 130.   [9] Ibid.

Müller says, by the following consideration. One cannot intend that V should be the case without the intention of doing something so that it should be the case; but where V is 'JMF's doing P', it is absurd to suggest that I, JMF (who have the intention to do P [or: of doing P]), have the intention of doing something so that V should be the case. (The suggestion involves embarking on an infinite regress.)

Now this shows why it is *possible* for me, when reasoning practically, to regard one mode of behaviour as better than an alternative without regarding the anticipated result of choosing the one as better than the result of choosing the other. The reason is: in reasoning practically I need not be considering my behaviour as a state of affairs (JMF doing P) at all. But this does not yet show what is wrong with the proportionalist or other eventistic claim that one should try to choose between results, i.e. between states of affairs. Müller offers an argument against that claim, but his argument needs supplementation.

The argument is that proportionalism (*qua* eventistic) seeks to guide choice by assessing states of affairs from a standpoint that anybody and everybody could occupy, an 'objective' standpoint (as opposed to the 'subjective' standpoint of the deliberating subject, the 'I' who am deliberating and choosing). Thus the proportionalist chooser seeks to stand above the world and choose between alternative possible worlds according to their respective amounts of value. So he might consider that Socrates doing a wrong and thus escaping execution is a better world than the world in which Socrates refuses to do wrong and suffers the greater wrong of being executed. But, says Müller, I am in reality not a demiurge, above the world, but a citizen of the world. So:

in real life it is inevitable that *at some point or other* I shall *no longer* acquire the criterion for my considered choice from the comparison of alternative eventistic possibilities in the face of a particular situation, since my choice . . . does itself modify the situation or the relationship of the alternatives one to the other (and it may do so relevantly).[10]

Now I think that Müller's objection is valid. At this point, however, imagination steps in to suggest that, in considering the value of the respective alternative possible worlds, one

---

[10] Ibid.

could somehow take fully into account the way in which the
respective possible worlds incorporate modifications created
or constituted by one's choice (e.g. the difference to character). But here imagination is playing tricks. My proof that it
is doing so does not rely on considerations such as I stressed
in the last chapter (IV.2): that the value of different traits of
character is really incommensurable with the value of other
aspects of states of affairs, and that it is just crazy to think
one can see and assess the value of future and hypothetical
states of affairs in anything like the manner suggested: the
effects of Socrates' refusal to participate in the liquidation of
Leon of Salamis are still substantial, 2,400 years later. No: to
prove that imagination is deceiving, when it suggests that I
can guide my own choice by an assessment of alternative
states of affairs which includes an evaluation of the difference made by my choosing itself, we need only consider the
following.

If one could do what imagination suggests, then one might
be assessing, say, four alternative possible states of affairs (I
here ignore the fact that the number of alternatives is not
rationally specifiable): (i) JMF does P on proportionalist
grounds and lives thereafter as a proportionalist; (ii) JMF
refuses to do P, and suffers the consequences; (iii) JMF refuses
to do P, and gets away with it; (iv) JMF does P, on proportionalist grounds, but thereafter *repents* of having done so
and lives according to a moral code such as Socrates'. And
this fourth alternative might very well be the best of those
four possible worlds. (Much of the argumentation in Hare's
Moral Thinking assumes that it might be so.) But that fourth
state of affairs is simply not a conceivable subject-matter
(object or content) of choice. I *cannot* conclude a train of
practical reasoning: 'P would be the *right* thing to do provided
I afterwards *repent* of having done P'. What might, on eventistic assumptions and in certain circumstances, seem the most
rational choice is, *as a choice*, merely irrational, incoherent.
Thus imagination's suggestion that I can reasonably consider
my own possible choices 'objectively', from a viewpoint that
anyone might adopt, must be a mere illusion.

Thus we see that Socrates' principle, when it identifies one
form of choice or action as *better* than another, is not
making a comparison of the value of those respective choices

or actions as states of affairs in possible worlds. 'Better', here, is to be read as 'reasonable as opposed to unreasonable'. Likewise, when Vatican II speaks of the wrongful choice being 'more degrading' to the chooser than to the victim, we must understand it as asserting that, in the perspective of practical reasoning (deliberation and choice), the unreasonableness of a choice is a more urgent and compelling consideration for the person who is choosing than are the harmful consequences of that person's choice for the person or persons who may have to suffer them. And this is not because practical reasonableness is the fetish of someone who wishes above all to cultivate his 'highest faculty', but simply because being practically reasonable is the way in which we can adequately respect and foster human well-being, and thus participate integrally in human goods (III.5)—indeed, for us who cannot bring about better worlds simply by surveying them from outside time and choosing them, it is the only way.

The arguments of this section have suggested grounds for holding, quite independently of the problem of incommensurability, that proportionalism cannot, i.e. logically cannot, do duty as a guide to practical reasoning, deliberation and choice. The ineligibility of proportionalism makes all the more urgent, however, the need to identify the genuine principle(s) by which Socrates, for example, could judge that participation in Leon's murder could not be other than wrongful. In other words, what is the *point* of abstaining from such participation, when it can be foreseen that abstention will probably not save Leon and will probably provoke yet another murder (of oneself)?

V.3   *'Treat humanity as an end, and never merely as a means'*

Kant was aware, I think, that proportionalism cannot be more than rationalization: 'Woe to those who creep through the serpent-windings of Utilitarianism' to avoid a categorical imperative and arrive at the conclusion they favour.[11] And he was vividly aware that choosing on a rational principle is

---

[11] Kant, *Metaphysische Anfangsgründe der Rechtslehre* (the first Part of his *Metaphysik der Sitten* (1796-7)), Part Two, Chap. I; trans. W. Hastie, *The Philosophy of Law . . . by Immanuel Kant* (Edinburgh: 1887), p. 195.

acting *for an end* but is not to be confused with making a rational judgment that one state of affairs is better than another. Moreover, his three formulations of the supreme principle of practical reasonableness—the three versions of the categorical imperative, versions which, with justified hesitations, he supposed were merely 'different formulations' of one fundamental principle—should be seen as a valuable attempt to identify the various intermediate principles which express the content and control the implications of the master principle of ethical reasoning (III.5), that one's choices should be open to human fulfilment. The first formulation of the categorical imperative,[12] we can say, excludes arbitrary self-preference in the pursuit of ends; the second[13] goes beyond that 'formal' requirement of universalization to require, 'materially', that *humanity*, whether in myself or in others, be respected in every action; and the third[14] demands, in effect, that ends be sought and found in community, in which each person's reasonable ends are treated as somehow ends for every other person and all such ends are thus harmonized in an ordered 'totality' or realm of personal ends.

Recent reflections on the possibility and content of a non-proportionalist ethic have concentrated on the second formulation of the categorical imperative. Rightly so, for Kant himself presents it as 'the supreme limiting condition in the pursuit of all means',[15] i.e. as the philosophical translation of the Pauline principle and as the supreme counter-principle to the proportionalist postulate that action is right when it is the most effective means to the producible state of affairs presumed to be proportionately best. Moreover, the second formulation of the categorical imperative is frequently used by Kant in discussing specific moral problems and is regarded by him as more than a mere side-constraint; it identifies not merely actions which must never be done, but also *positive* duties of self-cultivation and benevolence. Hence

[12] 'Act only according to that maxim by which you can at the same time will that it should become a universal law': Kant, *Grundlegung*, 421; trans. Beck, p. 44.

[13] 'Act so that you treat humanity, whether in your own person or in that of another, always as an end and never as a means only': *Grundlegung*, 429; trans. Beck, p. 54.

[14] Act according to a maxim which harmonizes with a possible realm (i.e. a systematic union of different rational beings through common laws) of ends as with a realm of nature: see *Grundlegung*, 436, 433; trans. Beck, pp. 62, 58.

[15] *Grundlegung*, 438; trans. Beck, p. 64.

we must consider whether Kant's 'Treat humanity as an end and never merely as a means' is to be preferred to the principle I formulated at the beginning of this chapter, 'Respect every basic human good in every one of your acts' or, more precisely, 'Do not choose directly against any basic human good'.

The difference between that last-mentioned principle and Kant's is no more and no less than this: Kant's conception of the 'humanity' which is to be respected in every act is restricted, fundamentally, to only one aspect of human flourishing or human nature. He insists on respect for other basic human goods, such as life, but only on account of their contribution to the maintenance and development of the one characteristic of human nature that we do not share with lower animals: rationality. 'Humanity', in the famous formula, means 'rational nature', i.e. the powers necessarily associated with rationality and 'the power to set ends' (i.e. free will or, in Kant's language, autonomy).

Here, indeed, we see that erratic block of Aristotelian argument (I.4) still rolling along through Western culture: the argument that *because* an aspect of human nature is not shared with other creatures, it ought to be the highest or even the exclusive object of ultimate human concern. In his recent reconstruction of Kant's fundamental ethics, Alan Donagan adopts that very argument and seems to place all his reliance on it.[16] Kant himself frequently insinuates the argument, but appeals also to quite different but equally dubious considerations based on his well-known philosophical methodology; in particular his view that moral philosophy cannot include any 'contingent', 'empirical' or 'anthropological' principles, i.e. principles not 'given a priori in pure practical reason'.[17]

The fact is that in his moral philosophy, as elsewhere, Kant has sought to correct and transcend the edifice of Humean philosophy without reshaping its building-blocks. In formulating the principle of respect for humanity or rational nature, Kant and Donagan rightly envisage a rational end (i.e. a that-which-gives-point-to-a-choice) which is not a state of

---

[16] Donagan, *The Theory of Morality*, p. 232.
[17] Kant, *Preface to the Metaphysical Elements of Ethics* (Part II of *Metaphysik der Sitten* [1797]), trans. T. K. Abbott, *Kant's . . . and other works on the Theory of Ethics* (3rd edn, London: 1883), p. 296.

affairs resulting from ('producible by') the chosen behaviour. Such an end transcends desire and inclination. In pursuing such an end, reason is not the slave of the passions; rather, reason is respecting and promoting itself. But, like Hume, both Kant and Donagan fail to observe that human understanding grasps *intelligible* ends, goods that are *understood*, not only in the capacity and activity of human rationality itself but also in other human possibilities and opportunities, other aspects of one's human nature.

Kant uses the categories 'human nature', 'perfection' and 'happiness', and gives them a proper architectonic role in his ethics. But he has evacuated them of all content save the power and activity of reason itself. The categorical imperative, he says, 'corresponds to' an end which is also a duty, an objective end. And there are two such ends: our own perfection, and the happiness of others (my own happiness is 'inevitably', by natural impulse, an end for me, and 'therefore' cannot be a matter of duty for me). But by happiness, Kant means no more than 'satisfaction with one's condition, with certainty of the continuance of this satisfaction'—a notion that uncritically embraces the body wallowing in the tank of the experience machine (II.3). And by perfection, Kant means 'nothing else than the *cultivation* of one's *power* (or natural capacity) and also of one's *will* (moral disposition) to satisfy the requirements of duty in general'. Cultivation of one's moral disposition to do one's duty is a matter of acquiring a certain feeling: 'a feeling of the effect which the legislative will within himself exercises on the faculty of acting accordingly'. Cultivation of one's natural capacity to do one's duty is a matter of 'raising himself more and more out of . . . his animal nature more and more to humanity'. But we have already seen that here, as in the famous second formulation of the categorical imperative, Kant means by 'humanity' no more than understanding and free rational choice, in short, rationality: the aspect of human nature that is above one's animal nature, an aspect that, in Kant's dualistic phrase, 'dwells within us'.[18]

Unfettered by the empiricist misunderstandings of human understanding (misunderstandings from which Kant never freed himself), our practical understanding easily grasps that

[18] All quotations in this paragraph are from ibid., pp. 295-8.

life, knowledge, play aesthetic appreciation, practical reasonableness, and friendship with one's fellows and one's maker
are each basic human goods, basic aspects of human flourishing (happiness, perfection). Kant sees in each of these (other
than practical reasonableness, which he elevates without
understanding its transparency for the other goods) no more
than the object of inclination, a movement of one's merely
empirical, contingent and indeed animal nature; to accord
these intrinsic significance in practical reasoning would be to
submit oneself to heteronomy (i.e. extrinsic constraints on
one's autonomy, one's self-determination). And if one were
to take the whole set as delineating a 'human nature' which
one sought to give status in practical reasoning by means of a
norm of the form 'Follow nature!', that too would be sub-
jection to heteronomy.

With this last point, I agree. But I add that besides Humean
and Suarezian conceptions of practical reasoning there is
the conception I have defended throughout these chapters.
The basic goods are no more and no less than *opportunities
of being all that one can be*. So far from being heteronomous,
they are, in fact, the *intrinsic point of one's autonomy*; they
outline the worthwhile 'self' that one may constitute by
one's self-determination, i.e. by the free choices towards
which all one's practical reasoning is directed. (On self-
determination, see VI.1.)

In short, if we read 'humanity' as including reference to all
the basic aspects of human flourishing, Kant's principle of
respect for humanity serves as a good and inspiring formulation of the master principle of ethical reasoning: make
one's choices open to human flourishing. His formulation
also conveys one of that master principle's specific implications: 'Respect each basic human good in each of your acts'.
But if we read 'humanity' as Kant explicitly meant it, we find
those intermediate principles of ethics conceived only 'thinly'
and with unjustified restrictions of content and scope.

V.4   *Respect every basic human good in each
of your acts*

The moral tradition constituted by the ethical *principles* of
Socrates and Plato, Aristotle and St Paul (and thus of St

Augustine and St Thomas) is commonly misunderstood. Contemporary critics of proportionalism, therefore, when formulating those principles of respect for persons which proportionalism undermines, find it convenient to name those principles 'Kantian'. The label can be accepted. But we must remain aware that what is valuable in Kant's ethics is what he shares with the tradition: a proper awareness that the moral goodness of a 'good will' (i.e. of a practically reasonable choice) is not—indeed, as we have seen (V.2), logically cannot be—assessable by assessing the overall value or disvalue of the states of affairs resulting from that choice.

And there is something else which the label 'Kantian' must not be allowed to obscure: when we fill out Kant's inadequate conception of the humanity that must be respected in every act, and identify basic goods intrinsic to humanity (and human perfection and happiness), we are not adulterating or diverging from the principle of respect for persons. We are simply treating persons in their non-dualistic wholeness.

The basic human goods, or values, are not mere abstractions; they are aspects—all the constitutive aspects—of the being and well-being of flesh and blood individuals. They are aspects of human personality.

Our fundamental responsibility is to respect each of those aspects, in each person whose well-being we choose (whether as end or as means) to affect. We never have sufficient *reason* to set aside that responsibility.

We often feel, or even 'have an intuition', that it is desirable to set aside that responsibility. But why such feelings and intuitions? Sometimes, they are a matter of sympathy with someone we know, and with whose feelings or fate we identify. But this sympathy, admirable in itself, needs chanelling and perhaps redirecting by intelligent reflection on the fate of the person against whose well-being, in some basic aspect, one is proposing directly to choose and act and who, therefore, falls more immediately within one's responsibility. Intelligent reflection will also disclose that in deliberate choosing, one ratifies, associates oneself with, and assents to other like choices in like situations (see VI.1); and that the likeness or unlikeness of situations cannot be limited or defined by the range and direction of one's own sympathies in one's own present situation.

At other times, or additionally, one's 'intuition' that it is right to choose directly against a basic good expresses, or results from, one's prior commitment to some project, community or institution. That prior commitment may have been, and may remain, entirely consistent with one's ultimate moral responsibility to favour integral human flourishing, and with the requirements of practical reasonableness that give shape to that master responsibility. But no such prior commitment or project is itself *required* by reason; at best the choice of commitment or project will have been *consistent* with all the requirements of practical reasonableness (IV.3). No project or commitment, therefore, can afford sufficient reason for overriding that intermediate principle of practical reasonableness which requires each person's well-being, in each of its basic aspects, to be respected—i.e. not chosen directly against—in every act.

In all cultures, the promptings of feelings and of prior projects and commitments will present themselves to the endlessly intellectualizing human mind as moral intuitions. And in a culture that has absorbed utilitarian or other proportionalist attitudes, those promptings will be represented (often quite sincerely) as expressions of, or consistent with, the demands of 'necessity', i.e. the necessity to achieve the proportionately greater overall net good, or to avoid the lesser net evil, in the situation. This is the process of rationalization which, as I said (IV.4), is logically inescapable whenever any attempt is made to arrive at a reasonable choice by an overall evaluation of alternative overall results of possible choices—inescapable because of (i) the contingency and indeterminacy of possible worlds, (ii) the incommensurability of basic goods and thus of measures for evaluating possible worlds, (iii) one's prior responsibility for one's own choices as an agent within the world, a responsibility which cannot be discerned from the demiurgic viewpoint adopted by proportionalist assessment. Proportionalism certainly adds respectability to the promptings of incompletely criticized feeling and of incompletely criticized loyalty to one's settled projects and commitments; respectability, but not rational justification.

What blocks acceptance of the principle of respect for persons (i.e. respect for basic human goods, in every act) is the high-sounding claim that each of us is fundamentally responsible for securing the overall greatest proportionate net good (or for preventing the greatest proportionate net evil) in every state of affairs and its presumed results. Once we have seen that this wildly misapprehends the master principle that every choice should favour and respect integral human well-being, we are left with no reasonable alternative to the principle of unconditional respect for persons. This is, indeed, the only principle on which any claim to inviolable human rights can be based. But it extends, as Kant noted, to require of me an unconditional respect for my own person, too.

V.5   *Can proportionalist weighing be avoided?*
         Punishment and self-defence

Here the proportionalist makes a last stand. He argues that the moral tradition itself regards an action 'as "turning directly against a basic good" only after the relation of the choice to all values has been weighed carefully':

An example will illustrate this. Finnis states: 'So, no suicide, no killing of the innocent: for human life is a fundamental value'. Why does he insert the word 'innocent'? After all, even the lives of the criminally guilty are fundamental values. The reason Finnis can insert the term 'innocent' and thus delimit those killings that involve a choice directly against a fundamental value is that he has first weighed the life of the criminal (or combatant, aggressor) against other possible competitive and more urgent values and decided that when a more urgent value (e.g. the common good) is threatened by a human life, then taking *that* life need not involve one in choosing directly against a basic value, regardless of the structure of the action involved. Is it not some such calculus that leads to the restriction 'innocent'?[19]

Or again:

On the basis of this and other forms of exception-making in the develop-ment of traditional norms, one has to conclude that a form of conse-quentialism cannot be excluded.[20]

But these claims are not made out. To formulate the norm 'Do not kill the innocent', neither the tradition nor my own thinking needed any consequentialist or other proportionalist 'weighing' or 'calculating'.

[19] McCormick, *Notes on Moral Theology*, p. 453 [1973].
[20] Ibid., p. 506 [1974]; verbatim in McCormick, *How Brave a New World?* (SCM Press, London: 1981) p. 157.

To see the reasoning that truly lies behind the traditional moral rules in question, begin with McCormick's own first example: punishment of criminals. Punishment has a point. But that point is not the sort of goal which utilitarians and consequentialists envisage; for they assume that the only rational point of choice is some resulting future state(s) of affairs involving the best proportion of pre-moral goods. But the defining and essential (though not necessarily the exclusive) point of punishment is to restore an order of fairness which was disrupted by the criminal's criminal act. That order was a fairly (it is supposed) distributed set of advantages and disadvantages, the system of benefits and burdens of life in human community. The disruption consisted in a choice to take the advantage of following one's own preferences rather than restraining oneself to remain within that fair order (or, where the crime is one of negligence, an unwillingness to make the effort required to remain within the legally or morally required pattern of actions and restraints). Since freedom to follow one's preferences is in itself an important human good, the criminal's act of self-preference was itself the gaining of an advantage over those who restrain themselves to remain within that legally and/or morally required pattern. So the essential point of punishment is to restore the disrupted order of fairness by depriving the criminal of his ill-gotten advantage. And since that advantage consisted at least primarily in (wrongful) freedom of choice and action, the appropriate means of restoring the order of fairness is by depriving the criminal of his freedom of choice and action.

Such is the traditional and, I believe, correct account of why a man's criminal guilt entitles certain persons (those with responsibility for maintaining the order of fairness in their community) to do actions which would otherwise amount to direct attacks on basic human goods in the person of the criminal. These acts of punishment may be useful for deterrence and reform and for maintaining public morale and for preventing vendettas, but none of those objectives entitle anyone to punish; the absolute pre-requisite for justified punishment is that there be a criminal and that the punishment be of the criminal and for his crime. Since, *pace* McCormick, the traditional account of punishment, and of occasions for suppressing life, was not consequentialist, that account rigorously excluded the hanging of a person known to be innocent by a sheriff confronting a murderous mob; the foreseeable good effects in terms of deterrence, prevention of riot, vendetta and murder, etc., count as nothing against the facts that the hanging of the innocent could not (i.e. logically could not) restore the order of fairness (since the innocent, *qua* innocent, had no ill-gotten advantage to be deprived of), and that the innocent, *qua* innocent, had not forfeited his right that basic goods be respected in his person.

You will notice that I am pointing up three features of the traditional and true account of the justification of punishment. *First*, there is the truth that actions can have a justifying point other than the creation of a state of affairs which, in terms of pre-moral goods, is proportionately better than alternatives. This truth is vigorously rejected by utilitarians and consequentialists of every stripe, who find the retributive theory of punishment simply the *pointless* creation of a bad state of affairs. (Those among them who are consistent also reject the ordinary human conceptions of gratitude and of praise, which are purely retributive conceptions; they have to say that we thank or praise a person not because he is entitled to it, nor because it is an intrinsically fitting response to a past good deed, but rather in order to encourage people to do good deeds in future. Thanks is for them merely a *means* of securing future benefits.)

Secondly, there is the truth that a person who violates the order of fairness, which can be described as a system of rights, forfeits certain of his own rights. That is to say, he loses the right that all others shall respect in his person all the basic aspects of human well-being. For those persons (and only those) whose responsibility it is to maintain the order of justice are now entitled to deprive him of certain of those basic goods, in order to restore the order of justice he disrupted. This act of deprivation will be, in one sense, an intentional attack on or suppression of basic human goods. But—and this is my *third* point—the deprivation or suppression will be intended neither for its own sake nor as a means to any further good state of affairs. Rather, it is intended precisely as itself a good, namely the good of restoring the order of justice, a restoration that cannot (logically cannot) consist

in anything other than such an act of deprivation or suppression.

The reasoning in the previous paragraph shows why even
capital punishment need not be regarded as doing evil that
good may come of it, nor as treating the criminal as a mere
means, nor as a choice which must be characterized as either
wholly or primarily an attack (however well motivated) on a
basic good. On the other hand, it does not show that capital
punishment is *required*, even for atrocious murders; part of
the traditional theory of punishment is that the measure of
just punishment is determined not by natural reason but
rather by positive (man-made) laws within the limits of
justice; so 'life for life' is not a requirement of reason. It may
also be that capital punishment, while not a direct attack on the
good of human life, displays an inadequate respect for that
good, except perhaps in those circumstances where no other
means are available to prevent further murderous or equivalently gross violations of justice by the criminal himself.

Thus the second and third points, above, remain applicable
even in the absence of the first. That is to say, the concepts
of forfeiting one's right to immunity from certain harms, and
of intending a harm not as an end nor as a means to any
further good state of affairs but simply as an act of justice,
are concepts applicable to justify a public officer (including
a policeman or soldier) deliberately inflicting harm, even
deadly harm, not by way of restoring the order of justice by
an act of punishment, but to protect the order of justice
against present or continuing criminal attack by the person so
harmed. Such an act is preventive, but not in the sense that
acts done for the sake of deterrence or reform or public satisfaction, etc., are preventive. This act protects the order of
justice by stopping a disruption of that order itself by the
person acted upon.

Throughout this discussion of the traditional theory of
the punitive and preventive rights of public officers, it is
important to bear in mind that the order of justice being
protected and/or rectified by the punitive and/or preventive
acts of those officers is an order that cannot (logically cannot) be disrupted by anything other than the unjust act (of
omission or commission) of the criminal. It is not an order
which is capable of being disturbed by someone's existence

or condition or location, even though that person's existence, state or location may be causing, or blocking the removal or prevention of, bad states of affairs such as a consequentialist or other proportionalist might seek to eliminate by eliminating that person. (The proportionalist can find no sufficient reason to rule out hanging the innocent to quell the fury of the mob; or blasting to pieces a child who got stuck in the entrance to a cave and whose body obstructs the exit of potholers fleeing rising flood waters; or killing the cabin boy in order to feed the other ship-wrecked sailors . . .) An intention to harm someone who is involuntarily endangering the welfare of others cannot be an act of justice, even when that harming of him would save others, even many others, from harm.

Aquinas speaks of killing justly inflicted deliberately by public officers for the sake of the common good. But by 'common good' he here means, not the proportionalist's future overall net welfare of the members of a community; rather, he means an order of rights and duties which are recognized and established to secure the welfare of each member of the community. That order is not, and logically cannot be, disturbed or disrupted by anything other than unjust human acts (of commission or omission); it is not disrupted by any other events or states of affairs, even when they constitute or result in the most grievous destruction of that communal welfare. An involuntary human act, since it involves no fault, is like an earthquake; it is not an act that disturbs or threatens the order of justice which it is the special responsibility of public officials to protect and restore. Thus Aquinas rules out all killing of the innocent, even when such killing would seem certain to secure the welfare of a community; for such killing could not be 'for the common good' as he uses that phrase and its equivalents. As he says, in this very context, 'it is not right to intend any harm to anyone except by way of punishment for the sake of justice' (or, we may add, for the sake of preserving justice by stopping an act which, if completed, would be worthy of punishment).[21]

The traditional formulation which McCormick thinks needs a consequentialist justification is usually formulated

[21] *Summa Theologiae* I-II, q. 65, a. 2c; see also Aquinas, *in II Sent.*, dist. 42, q. 1, a. 2c.

thus: 'Do not directly kill the innocent'. I have shown that the use of the word 'innocent' owes nothing to consequentialist considerations. But what about the word 'directly'? Does that covertly appeal to a proportionalist concern for overall long-term pre-moral good?

No, the word 'direct' sums up a set of non-proportionalist considerations concerning the situation of (a) public officers confronted by an involuntary human threat to the life or safety of other human beings, and (b) private persons confronted by a voluntary or involuntary threat to their own life or safety. Anyone so confronted is morally entitled to repel the threat, to stop it in its tracks, by means sufficient (but no more than sufficient: here is a genuine traditional use of 'proportionate') to stop it even if those means will as a matter of fact cause the death of the person whose act (however involuntary) is *itself* the threat. The act of self-defence is, to use the famous and rather unfortunate phrase, an act with a double effect; one effect is the stopping of the life-threatening act, the other is the bringing about of the death of the attacker. For the one engaged in justified self-defence, the latter effect is a side-effect and so can be unintended; and where death is an unintended and unwanted result of an act otherwise justifiable, there is no direct killing and no choice directly against the basic good of life, no doing evil for the sake of good and no treating of the humanity of the attacker as a mere means to any end.

Some contemporary moral theorists who reject all forms of proportionalism consider that killing is only justifiable where it is the side-effect of a justifiable act of stopping a life-threatening attack. But I think these theorists here overlook the unique modality of intention and of personal responsibility (including liability-responsibility) which becomes possible when a fair order of rights and duties is established in a community and administered by persons who therefore have a public role quite distinct from their private rights and duties. So I think that private self-defence is only one of the two great paradigm cases of what can loosely be called justifiable killing, the other paradigm case being the act of the public officer deliberately killing as a lawful and justified act of upholding punitively or quasi-punitively the order of justice in his community. Still, whichever of these non-proportionalist views is adopted, there is here no attempt, even covertly, to justify any killing by looking to the balance of pre-moral goods and bads in any state of affairs; the terms 'direct' and 'innocent' do not relate to any such balancing or pursuit of 'greater good' or 'lesser evil'.

The paradigms of punishment and self-defence must be contrasted with the paradigm of consequentialist or proportionalist killing, where the 'common good' (now used in a proportionalist sense as overall net future general welfare) is secured against the threats of enemies or natural calamities by deliberately killing bystanders who are innocent both in terms of the punishment paradigm (because they are not culpably threatening anyone themselves) and in terms of the self-defence paradigm (because they themselves are doing nothing to threaten anyone). The traditional moralist reveals the non-proportionalist bases of his 'formulations' when, without illusion about the evil purposes of our enemies, he condemns any act, even by statesmen, soldiers or other public officials, that seeks to destroy innocent civilians of the enemy's country. He condemns such acts even when they would be the indispensable means of persuading the enemy to desist from his criminal attack and thus of averting our own defeat or destruction.

What sort of conception of personal responsibility, and ultimate destiny, underlies so drastic and 'unpractical' a practical judgment (and all the other practical judgments with which it is consistent)? Parts of the answer to that question have been given in this and earlier chapters. But those parts need to be drawn together, and more remains to be said. To that I now turn.

NOTES

V.1

Proportionalism is not coherent with belief in providence... See Germain Grisez, *The Way of the Lord Jesus*, vol. I, chap. 6, quest. F; G. de Broglie, 'Malice intrinsèque du péché et péchés heureux par leur conséquences' (1934) 24 *Recherches de Science Religieuse*, 302 at pp. 303–9. Theological proportionalists sometimes deny that their ethical method ascribes to human beings the responsibilities of God. But their injunction to use overall long-run consequences (whether 'at large' or in their bearing, through 'associated goods', on the good 'at stake') has no intrinsic limits.

V.2

Müller's argument against eventism . . . For its roots in his study of the first person, see his 'Reply to "I"', Khanbai, Katz and Pineau, *Jowett Papers 1968-1969* (Blackwell, Oxford: 1970), 11-22. My own discussion of the argument against eventism owes much to private debate with Joseph Raz.

The set of alternative states of affairs open to rational choice is not exhaustively specifiable . . . See Lars Bergström, 'Utilitarianism and Alternative Actions' (1971) 5 *Noûs*, 237; Dan W. Brock, 'Recent Work in Utilitarianism' (1973) 10 *American Philosophical Q.* 241 at 249-50; Geach, *The Virtues*, pp. 103-4. Hare, *Moral Thinking*, p. 95n, protests that this problem is not peculiar to utilitarianism; he forgets that there are ethical methods which do not claim to identify the one *right* answer, and which do not pretend that wrong choices are identifiable by determining what choices would not yield better consequences than any available alternative choices. The methods overlooked by Hare are not uninterested in 'rational choice'; but they keep cost-benefit calculations in their (subordinate) place.

V.3

'Treat humanity . . . never as a means only' versus 'Do not choose directly against a basic good' . . . Cf. Donagan, *The Theory of Morality*, pp. 61-6, preferring the former to the latter. For the interpretation of 'humanity' in Kant's formula, see Thomas E. Hill, Jr, 'Humanity as an End in Itself' (1980) 91 *Ethics*, 84 at p. 86.

Suarezian conceptions of practical reasoning . . . See Finnis, *Natural Law and Natural Rights*, pp. 54-5, 336-43, 347, 350. An interesting, and by no means unique or uninfluential, marriage of Suarezian with Kantian misunderstandings of practical reasonableness is to be found in Karl Rahner's later writings. Here the fundamental moral norm is conceived in Suarezian terms: 'Follow, or respect, nature'. But in that norm, 'nature' is interpreted as a Kantian 'transcendental nature', i.e. those 'objective structures of human nature which are . . . implicitly affirmed by a transcendental necessity even in the act of their denial'. The 'denial' envisaged here is an *'explicit'* denial; even suicide 'does nothing to deny the transcendental necessity of man's nature': Rahner, 'The Problem of Genetic Manipulation' [1968], in his *Theological Investigations*, vol. 9 (Darton, Longman and Todd, London: 1972), p. 231; so the 'transcendentality' in question is simply man's 'free, subjective self-awareness' (ibid., p. 232); the transcendental nature that must be respected is no more than man's 'essence', i.e. 'the personal spirit . . . in freedom and radical self-possession . . .' (ibid., p. 215). (Man's 'essence' is often contrasted by Rahner with mere 'concrete human nature': see *Theological Investigations*, vol. 14 (London: 1976) pp. 15–16; also *Lexicon für Theologie und Kirche*, Bd. 7, col. 827.) Rahner adds that 'All the same (and not least since it constitutes authoritative Church teaching) the doctrine of the unity of body and spirit (soul) compels us to maintain a very intimate connection between man's transcendental nature and his biological constitution': *Theological Investigations*, vol. 9, p. 233. But his Suarezian and Kantian ethical methodology leaves him no way of according significance to that 'intimate connection' in his ethical reasoning. The dualism in Rahner's notion of human nature, though very significant, need not be considered here.

V.5

The traditional theory of the justification of punishment . . . See Aquinas, *Summa Theologiae* I-II, q. 87, a. 6c; *Summa contra Gentiles* III, c. 140, para. 5; c. 146, para. 1.

Capital punishment need not be regarded as a direct attack on human life . . . My discussion here is a reply to the arguments in Grisez, 'Towards a Consistent Natural Law Ethics of Killing' (1970) 15 *American J. Jurisprudence*, 64 at pp. 67-70.

VI
Ethics and our Destiny

VI.1 *The significance of free choices*

If scepticism were justified, really caring about anything would be unintelligible—not impossible, but unintelligible and therefore, apparently, unintelligent. Scepticism about the basic forms of human flourishing, and about the fundamental requirements of practical reasonableness, is therefore the foremost threat to ethics, and was the main theme of Chapters II and III.

My second theme has been proportionalism. The proportionalist claims that we must care about everything that we *could* affect by our choices: everything that I could affect by my choices is within my responsibility, and I must not fail to do everything I can to maximize *overall* net good, *on the whole* and in the *long run*. The logically necessary implication of this high-sounding doctrine is to abolish care for the *rights* of those weak and innocent whose very existence impedes the (supposed) overall proportionately greater good which is meant to be the exhaustive object of my care. The rationally necessary effect of the doctrine is rationalization, which compromises between the impossible pursuit of overall net good and as many conventional moral standards as a proportionalist is willing to retain from the culture he admires. Thus he preserves himself from the otherwise inevitable psychological effect of shouldering responsibility for everything: collapse of any principled moral concern for anything.

So proportionalism threatens ethics by asserting a criterion of moral judgment which makes moral choice ultimately insignificant. What matters is, only, the overall net good. My attempts to secure that good interact with other people's efforts, and with their indifference and hostility, and with the whole play of chance and contingency, in nature and in human activity alike. My most solemn moral choices may well have less influence on the world-historical outcome than my most accidental stumble or my decision to have another cup of coffee before going off to work. For want of a nail . . . the kingdom was lost . . .

Thus, each in its own way, scepticism and proportionalism denude our free choices of significance. It is fitting now to consider, therefore, what significance free choice (as a fact and as an opportunity) has for practical reasonableness, i.e. for ethics.

But first: are there any free choices? By 'free choice' I mean this: a choice is free if and only if it is between open practical alternatives (i.e. to do this, or to do that . . .) such that there is no factor but the choosing itself which settles which alternative is chosen.

Belief that there are some free choices is neither logically incoherent nor contrary to immediate experience. Belief that there are no free choices must therefore be argued for. But since such an argument can rely neither on immediate experience nor logical incoherence, it must appeal to a norm of rationality (e.g. the alleged principle of sufficient reason). Now although norms of rationality prescribe unconditionally, refusal to adhere to them in one's thinking and judging is physically and psychologically possible. For to say that they prescribe unconditionally is to say that rejection of them (and of the conclusions rationally based upon them) is not open *to a person committed to the rational pursuit of truth*; but it is logically, physically and psychologically possible not to be committed to the rational pursuit of truth. Thus the rational affirmation of the view that there are no free choices is possible only for one who chooses between the open alternatives of (i) adhering to the rationality norms appealed to by those who argue that there are no free choices, or (ii) refusing to adhere to those rationality norms. But such a choice between open alternatives is, by definition, a free choice. Thus: to argue for the view that there are no free choices is self-defeating.

Notice, incidentally, another instance of the epistemological priority of ethics (or, at least, of practical reasoning) in any study of human nature. Free choice can only be understood and affirmed by one who understands that the chooser really did confront what I have called *open alternatives*. The openness of alternatives is to be understood not by reflection on the situation of a rat or a man at a junction in a maze, or of an ass or a man confronted with two appetizing foods. Rather, it is to be understood by reflection on the experience of deciding between two *intelligible* goods: say, the good of obtaining and seriously studying a worthwhile book on ethics, at the cost of $20, and the good of giving that $20 to a genuine charity. And that intelligibility of these two incommensurable goods, and of the rational principles to which one might choose to adhere in acknowledging these two as worthy uses of the $20, is an intelligibility grasped first in practical reasoning itself. Free choice could not rationally be affirmed in anthropology or metaphysics were there not an experience of free choice. But that experience is not of something happening to oneself; rather it is the experience of doing something, i.e. of *praxis*. And in the first instance, it is the experience of confronting alternatives grasped by practical understanding as goods.

Free choice, in the sense I am speaking of, was far from being denied by Plato or Aristotle. The early Christian philosophers, who first made free choice and self-determination a philosophical theme (calling for a new term: *autexousia*), were able plausibly to claim Plato as their·forerunner in this recognition. I think we should say, however, that neither Plato nor Aristotle nor any other Greeks recognized free choice for what it is: something far more than absence of external constraint or compulsion. And in due course, having fallen under suspicion in the Reformation, free choice came to be denied by the mainstream of the Enlightenment and of modern thought. To affirm that there are some free choices is to deny what many suppose is required by science or philosophy (though, as we have just seen, this supposition is literally indefensible); it is to affirm that sometimes I choose between alternatives that are open, in the sense that there is no factor, not even a 'system of preferences' of mine or 'set of wants' of mine, which *settles* which alternatives I choose. Thus it is to affirm that some at least of our choices are genuinely *creative*, precisely because they are not merely the product of anything that was already 'there' (my existing wants, preferences, habits . . .).

A free choice, therefore, is already—even before its

execution in action begins—a realization of the basic human good(s) for the sake of which the choice was made. Or, if the choice was morally bad, it is *already* a diminution of the basic good(s) attacked or irrationally neglected in that choice. To recognize that there are some free choices is to recognize that choice and action have both transitive and intransitive effects. The transitive effects of choice and action are the states of affairs constituted by my chosen behaviour and its further results in the world. The intransitive effect is this: by a free choice I willy-nilly constitute myself a certain sort of person. By choosing to go home rather than set off with the other four to liquidate Leon of Salamis, Socrates constituted (or reconstituted), established (or re-established) himself as a certain kind of person, as a respecter of human life and of the Rule of Law, as one who rejects lawless murder and retains his autonomy against pressures to become a pawn of tyrants . . .

This intransitive, self-determining effect and creative significance of choice can be better understood by considering its further dimension. Choices *last*. What choices create is not merely some new wants, preferences, habits . . ., but also a new (not wholly new) identity or character. All free choices last in the sense that they change the person (even though he will remain someone who in future can make choices which are free because not *determined* by his wants, preferences, habits, or previous choices). One way of expressing this lasting of free choices is found in sayings like: 'As a result of my choice to do X, I am committed to doing XA, but not because XA is a means to X, nor because X was a promise or undertaking to anyone, even myself . . ., and not merely because X changed my circumstances . . .' (The more strategic or architectonic the choice of X, the greater the degree of commitment and the more substantial the lasting of that choice.) This sort of commitment is the counterpart in my will (i.e. in my identity as a chooser between rationally open alternatives) of the 'logic' of universalization in practical reasoning. Not that this sort of commitment destroys free choice. One can choose to do what one was committed not to do . . ., by acting unreasonably, inconsistently . . . But one cannot (logically cannot) *escape* from this sort of commitment except by *repenting of* (in a strong sense; not merely regretting) one's former choice.

Choices last until an incompatible choice is made. A choice to make a more or less formal 'act of repentance', with an explicit inward or outward expression of one's contrition and of one's resolve not to repeat one's now-repudiated choice, is one form of such an incompatible subsequent choice, but I use the term 'repent' to refer to any such incompatible subsequent choice. Thus: My former choice was an act by which, willy-nilly, I who was choosing constituted myself as the person I thenceforth was and still, unless I have repented of it, am.

This shaping of the person is, if you like, the creation (or strengthening or destruction or replacement) of a disposition, a virtue or a vice. But if we are to use those classical words in this context, we must insist on their very strong sense; they denote realities that are created by, and in this sense only by, acts of self-determination (free choices) and that are superseded and replaced only by a subsequent incompatible act or acts of free choice.

To speak of choices lasting in this way is to speak of a reality of which one can certainly be more or less aware, and about which one can make reasonable and true affirmations, but which cannot itself be isolated as an 'observable datum' of direct experience for investigation by the methods of the natural sciences. In this respect, the reality of free choices and their lasting is like that other notably spiritual yet equally commonplace reality: the acts of understanding and judgment which constitute one a knower. Knowledge is more than its empirical and experiential concomitants, such as memory and recall; it actually shapes one's whole stance as a questioner and affirmer, by determining what sort of questions one would take seriously, what one would count as evidence, and so on . . . So too, free choices create more than the experienced inclinations and (in the modern sense of the word) habits which accompany and/or result from them. One's character takes the shape of the choice one has made.

As I have said, universalizability (or, more simply, consistency) is not just a logical property of, or logical constraint upon, moral norms (or other items of meaning) qua meanings: to say 'He did X, and so he is committed to doing XA' expresses a truth not only about the relation between the practical propositions 'X is to be done' and 'XA is to be done', but also about the person who chose to put the first of those practical propositions into practice.

This lastingness of unrepented choices is the counterpart, in one's spirit or character, of the rational (not merely moral) requirement of *diachronic* universalization of one's choices: the requirement that one's later choices be consistent with one's earlier unrepudiated choices. (And universalization, in turn, is an entailment of the fact that choice is between *understood* goods: II.2, II.5 above.) I cannot, in reason, say to myself 'X is the right, or the reasonable, thing to do here and now, but I won't ever do it again'. When one says, 'I won't do X again if I get out of here alive', one either means 'I know that I shouldn't be doing X here and now . . .', or one means 'I'll make sure I never again get into a situation where choice of something like X is the reasonable choice'; and expressions of the latter sort are often self-deceiving or, at least, mere wishful thinking. The principles or methods of evaluation (whether moral or not) which one used in identifying X as the right thing to do, here and now, are principles applicable in like fashion to other situations; usually they will be applicable, like it or not, to *many* future situations. (They are applicable, too, in relation to the past; by one's practical judgment and choice one is committed to passing judgment in a particular fashion on the choices and deeds of everyone who was ever in like situation.) Nothing short of repentance, a subsequent new and incompatible act of choice, will free one from the implications of one's former decision to follow those principles. For those implications were not merely logical; they traced the shape of what one willy-nilly, by one's earlier choice, determined oneself to be.

Thus one's free choices, whether of particular acts, or of complex projects, or of overarching commitments, constitute one the sort of person—indeed, *the* person—one has made oneself. But when we think of self-determination, self-constitution and self-realization, we must be careful to recall that constant theme of these chapters: the transparency of practical deliberation and choice. Self-constitution is a foreseeable, intrinsic and necessary effect of one's free choices, but it is not, typically, a motivating reason for any choice. The choice to go home rather than go to Salamis established Socrates as a just man, a respecter of human life and upright in the face of tyrants. But being a man of such character was a good thing *just to the extent that* the choice that constituted him such a man was *itself a good and reasonable choice*.

What motivated Socrates' choice was respect for Leon as a living human person, and for the lawful order of Greek justice. And those motives are sufficient and complete reason for his choice. Socrates could *reflect* that his choice would preserve his own good character or, as the vulgar cynic would have it, 'keep his hands clean'. But these would indeed be reflections, not motivating thoughts or reasons for the choice. One can affirm and approve the 'state of the self' that one constitutes and confirms by one's choice, without that state of the self being in any way one's objective. (So too one can regret and detest the character one has chosen, without choosing to repent and reform around some new principle of self-integration.)

VI.2   *A fundamental option to be reasonable?*

Some people imagine that one's moral life is structured by a fundamental option between, say, being reasonable (upright, just . . . etc.) and being unreasonable or selfish or one who refuses the opportunities open to him . . . But there seems to be no evidence that such fundamental options are made. What passes as evidence turns out to be questionably metaphorical: there is talk, for example, of 'the depths of the soul, where a man is totally present to himself' and where he performs an act of 'fundamental liberty' that is not a choice to do or abstain from doing anything in particular but is 'rather the free determination of oneself with regard to the totality of existence and its direction . . . a fundamental choice between love and selfishness . . .'[1]

I do not doubt that in choosing one can be more or less recollected, more or less 'self-conscious', i.e. conscious of one's mixed motives, more or less serious and seriously committed. But I can see no sense in talk of a self which (while

---

[1] McCormick, *Notes on Moral Theology*, p. 71 [1967]; McCormick, 'The Moral Theology of Vatican II' in *The Future of Ethics and Moral Theology* (Argus, Chicago: 1968), p. 12.

not doing or considering doing anything in particular?) is totally present to itself, and which at the same time determines itself by a choice which is not a choice to *do* anything at all. These supposed transactions of selves with themselves, in a 'presence' to themselves which is said to be both 'total' and 'deeply mysterious', are all too reminiscent of Thomas Nagel's 'true self' viewing the world 'through' the person of Thomas Nagel 'as through a window' (III.3 above). (One source of these imaginings about the self is traced by Anscombe to oversight of one form of what I call transparency, viz. the fact that 'I' is neither a name nor any other kind of expression whose logical role is to make a *reference*.)[2]

And how could a 'fundamental choice' of this supposed sort be made? Whenever we choose anything, we choose it because it seems to offer some good, some intelligible advantage or opportunity. But what intelligible advantage could anyone see in being selfish rather than loving, or unreasonable rather than reasonable, *apart from the advantages offered by some particular objective, or some particular option for action by him*?

No. One chooses to be selfish and unreasonable in the free choices one makes to do a selfish and unreasonable act, just as the four who went off to Salamis chose to be murderers and pawns of tyrants by choosing to set out for Salamis to participate in Leon's liquidation. Doubtless, they made some effort to rationalize their choice as an exceptional 'necessity'. Doubtless, they would have sought to persuade themselves not only that they were not making themselves selfish, unjust, unreasonable or immoral, but also, and more vehemently, that they were not making any fundamental option for any of those unattractive characteristics. (Who indeed would ever *choose* or embrace any of those characteristics, in the depths of his soul or anywhere else?) But unless and until they repudiated their act as not merely regrettable and 'tragic' but actually wrongful (their own wrong), they were what they had made themselves by their free choice: unjust, murderous . . .

I do not deny that there are complications. People can be inconsistent. Duress can, at the limit, impair the freedom of one's choice. And when it is a question of assessing culpability, circumstances can confuse the issue of choice and thus be

<hr />

[2] *The Collected Philosophical Papers of G. E. M. Anscombe*, vol. II, p. 32.

extenuating. But my purpose is not to assign blame, but to point out that each serious and deliberate choice, made with awareness of what is being chosen, and directly affecting a basic human good, is itself a fundamental option for or against practical reasonableness or, if you prefer, against virtue. It is fundamental because it makes a change in the self by which all future choices will be made, whether reasonably (virtuously) or unreasonably (wrongly).

Such changes certainly differ in degree. The 'fundamental' options of which I am speaking are more and less architectonic or strategic, and one's self-integration around the principle of one's choices always remains incomplete in this life. But the fact remains: each serious option is fundamental precisely because one's character is reconstituted and re-formed around that choice, and because that choice will last, i.e. will remain a constitutive of one's personality, character, self . . . until, if ever, one chooses equally deliberately and freely to repent of it.

VI.3   *Objectivity and friendship revisited*

A reflection on *lasting* suggests, inescapably, a reflection on *passing*. And this in turn provokes a reflection on the wider order in which all our choices are set.

My participation in human goods, and yours, not only lasts (in my character, as well as in my acquired 'technical' skills, and in the transitive effects of my acts and omissions). It also, in many respects, passes away as health fails, as things once known become forgotten, as forms of play and exercises of skill slip beyond our capacities or lose their savour, as friendships are ended by separations and deaths. We may perhaps see these goods being participated in with full vigour by our children and by other members of our various communities. But we know that even the most flourishing communities of the past have suffered shipwreck, sometimes with awful suddenness and completeness. We each take our place, then, as individuals in a great succession of communities; but the word 'succession' cannot mask the fact that both time and space seem to separate us utterly from countless individuals and communities who have participated in human good and then passed away. So the question arises whether there is indeed a more universal order in which we do significantly take our place, and in relation to which our choices for good have a wider significance than we now see in them or attribute to them.

And as we look beyond the succession of persons and their communities to the whole universe of entities and states of affairs, indefinitely extended in space and time, we can ask whether it, too, has a point or value—and whether it has any bearing on my good, or the good of any other human person or community.

Such questions go beyond a recognition that 'human good' is an anthropocentric category, i.e. one of the many categories which are what they are because human observers and thinkers and doers are as they are (III.3). Rather such questions ask whether human goods are of *merely* anthropocentric significance. And from what I have just said about the evident *separation* between each of us (and each of our communities) and countless other human beings, it follows that if human goods are of merely anthropocentric significance then the significance of my participation in human goods, and yours, the significance of my choices and yours, is really very restricted. In this perspective, the claims upon us of the basic principles and requirements of practical reasonableness will seem to have a debilitating subjectivity—not the subjectivity alleged by the sceptics who deny the reality of practical understanding and the rationality of practical reasonableness, but the subjectivity of the '*merely* relative to us' (where 'us' has an uncertain but fairly narrow extension).

If that is indeed the situation, then we must put up with it and not seek comfort in myths and stories which pretend that things are otherwise.

But, as I have argued more fully elsewhere,[3] there are reasons for thinking that that is not our situation. For our explanations of states of affairs in this world are radically insufficient unless there is one state of affairs whose existing is a prerequisite for the existing of all other states of affairs, but whose existing does not require any prerequisite condition, not included in that state of affairs itself. Such a state of affairs could be called an uncaused causing, and its own existing would be explained by the fact that it includes

[3] *Natural Law and Natural Rights*, ch. XIII.

within itself a state of affairs, 'D', that exists simply because of what it is. We know of no other state of affairs such that *what* it is is all that it requires to exist, no other state of affairs such that to state what it is is to state *that* it exists. Even D's uncaused causing of all other states of affairs is a state of affairs that might or might not have existed. And this is the basis for the philosophical speculation that D's causing of all other states of affairs, being an uncaused causing which determines between contingent possibilities, is somehow analogous to human free choices.

For we, by our freely chosen acts of thinking, choosing, using or making, bring into being entities and states of affairs (arguments, friendships, poems, performances, constitutions . . .) that simply would not exist but for our not-wholly-determined acts. Thus D's uncaused causality can be described as an *act*, and can be thought of as presupposing something like our *knowledge* of the alternative possibilities available to be brought to realization by choice and creation —i.e. our practical knowledge of those possibilities as *opportunities*. But if D thus acts and knows, our conception of D's existing can employ the model of *personal life*.

These philosophical speculations about the character of D's existing cannot, so far as I can see, be established with philosophical certainty. But the conclusion that D exists and is an uncaused cause can be affirmed with philosophical certainty.[4] So it is reasonable to suppose that, if D's existing is a kind of personal existing, some sort of communication from, or self-disclosure of, D might occur. Whether it does occur is not a question for philosophy; it is a question of (historical) fact.

Philosophy, and in particular ethics, can, however, say something about what might be the significance of the relationship(s) that might be possible between each of us and that being, D, if D's personal life were sufficiently disclosed to us by D's revelatory initiative.

The ethics of Plato and Aristotle are in no way closed to the divine. But they do not envisage a fully personal relationship between human beings and the God. In part this is because they do not envisage creative causality in its sheer creativity, i.e. in its full freedom from all pre-determining

---

[4] Ibid., pp. 382-7.

materials or forces (fate . . .); hence they do not *clearly* envisage the existence of the God as a personal life, nor do they clearly acknowledge that the God's creative choice is the explanatory source not only of the orderliness and beauty (the measure . . .) of all good things and states of affairs but also of their very existing, their very possibility of existing.

What should we say to Aristotle's opinion that God is too remote to be our friend? The first thing to say is that a full understanding of D's (or God's) utter independence of any preconditions or prerequisites for D's creative causality—i.e. of D's utter self-sufficiency, and transcendence in relation to all other states of affairs whatsoever—tends of itself to underline and reinforce our sense of D's (or God's) remoteness. Our own utter dependence upon D's causality amounts, of course, to a kind of immediacy of D to us *qua* creatures being caused by D here and now. But the same utter dependence makes us almost incomparably remote from D *qua* uncreated and absolutely independent.

The second thing to say is that D's remoteness from us is a matter of fact. If, as a matter of fact, D chooses to communicate to us some understanding of D's personal life, and of the goods that D 'had (or has) in mind' in creatively causing our world and our opportunities, then, as a matter of fact, we may be entitled to find D's concerns not so remote from ours. And there is no reason to doubt that the 'available facts' may well be different, and richer, now than in Aristotle's time and milieu.

Thirdly: to respond to Aristotle's opinion on this point, we need to have clear our ideas of friendship, i.e. of the paradigm case of friendship between two human beings. In that sense of the word 'friendship', A is the friend of B when (i) A acts (or is willing to act) for B's well-being, for the sake of B, while (ii) B acts (or is willing to act) for A's well-being, for the sake of A, and (iii) each of them knows of the other's activity and willingness, and of the other's knowledge, and (iv) each of them co-ordinates (at least some) of his or her activity with the activity (including acts of friendship) of the other—so that there is a sharing, community, mutuality and reciprocity not only of knowledge but also of activity (and thus, normally, of enjoyment and satisfaction). Now, when we say that A and B act 'for the sake of' each other, we mean that the concern of each for the other is founded, not in devotion to some principle according to which the other, as a member of a class picked out by that principle, is entitled to concern, but rather in regard or affection for that individual person as such.

Pausing to review the concept of friendship at this point in the analysis, we can see that all parts of it, save one, are conceivably applicable, in some form, to a relationship between God and any human being to whom God has made sufficient disclosure of His personal life and concerns. What is inapplicable is any notion that a human being could act 'for God's well-being'. For the one thing we know with certainty about D, and thus about God, is that D lacks nothing that could be required for D to exist and to cause all that does and could exist. Still, it remains possible for me as a human being to act 'for the sake of God', i.e. out of regard and affection for God as such, and out of concern that God's concerns be advanced, i.e. that the goods that God favours and chooses should be favoured and chosen by me, out of friendship. Since we know that God needs and lacks nothing, we are forced to regard God's creative activity as essentially a kind of play—a free but patterned expression of life and activity, meaningful though with no point beyond itself, yet in no way frivolous, but rather a glorious manifestation of the goodness of the source of all goods whatever. Thus any friendship with God must be regarded as a sharing, in a limited way, in the divine play—a sharing already envisaged, in a particular form, by Plato,[5] as the only really serious thing to be concerned with.

Such a friendship with God would relativize our self-love and would dispel the anxiety that most insidiously undermines any and every ethics, the anxiety that concern to be practically reasonable (virtuous, upright . . .) is ultimately no more than a refined form of self-cultivation.

That anxiety would be allayed, because every form of genuine friendship relativizes our self-love without destroying or discrediting it. Friendship between A and B is a good for A (an aspect of his flourishing) and a good for B, too. But, to be a friend, A must act substantially for B's good (not for his own, A's) and must value B's good for the sake of B (rather

[5] *Laws* VII, 803b–c.

than for the sake of what he, A, can get out of the friendship); in other words, A must treat B's own good as an aspect
of his (A's) own good. Yet, at the same time, B must value
A's good for the sake of A, and treat A's good as an aspect
of his (B's) own good. It follows that A, for the sake of B,
must value his (A's) own good. In the eyes of his friend A,
B's good is transparent for A's good, which in turn is transparent for B's . . . And thus (to shift the metaphor) the
reciprocity of concern, friendship, love . . . does not come to
rest at either pole. Self-love is not destroyed, but is taken up
into a new perspective in which one is no longer acting
exclusively for one's own sake (or from one's own point of
view) nor exclusively for one's friend's sake (or from his or
her point of view); rather, one is acting for a good that is
truly common.

And much of this dialectic of friendship seems applicable
in principle to the postulated friendship between God and
man. Certainly, one cannot act for God's good, for God's
well-being. But one could act, out of love for God, for the
sake of favouring the goods that God favours, goods which
include one's own good as well as the good of all other
human persons. And thus one's concern to be practically
reasonable would not need to be regarded either as a search
for self-perfection or self-cultivation, or as obedience to
sheer categorical imperatives unrelated to any participation
in intelligible good(s). Rather, it could be seen as what is
needed to participate in the play of God, to favour and
participate integrally in the human goods, which God's
creative activity (subject to our free choice so to favour and
participate in them) makes possible.

We may add that it would indeed be surprising if the God
whose creative causality makes human friendships possible
(by making lovable human persons) turned out to love
human persons with less than the love that we can find
possible for one or more of our human fellows, or with less
than the respect that we find it reasonable to accord to the
basic human goods in every other human being.

It will be objected that this God is responsible for the evils
and disorders of this world. In the last analysis, this should
not be denied. For while D does not cause evils precisely as
such (since evil is a lack, a defect, the non-existing of what

ought to exist . . .), still D creates all the states of affairs that involve evil. But we cannot judge that D's causality is itself evil or defective. For we do not know what the norms applicable to creative causality are. Thus it remains possible that the terms of God's self-disclosure to us could provide sufficient grounds for us to respect, honour and love God, even by the standards by which we assess human situations as good and bad, standards which no doubt somehow mirror, but only to some extent, the norms or standards of creative causality (the norms called, in the language of Augustine and Aquinas, the Eternal Law).

Finally, there is no need to labour the point that if God were revealed as the cause of all human goods, and as offering the gift of friendship with all human beings of every time and place, this fact would eliminate the subjectivity of which I spoke at the beginning of this section—the subjectivity of goods that seem merely relative to us, as individuals and communities apparently cut off from the goods and ills of countless other individuals and communities and from vast parts of a universe whose overall point we do not grasp. For, on the hypothesis that I am considering, we could be confident that the participation in human good(s) that we can realize by our own free choices is a good which will indeed 'have a place' and 'have a point' in the overall pattern and common good of the created universe—a pattern and common good not now understood by us, but understood and chosen by the same God who is responsible for all the goods that we can, at least partly, understand and value.

VI.4   On 'the last things'

Philosophy cannot disclose that any human relationship with God will last beyond death. But it can say something about the significance of that possibility. Here I shall add two points to what is obviously implied in what I have already said about the possibility of friendship with God.

In the first place, philosophy can point out the almost paradoxical nature of self-determination through free choices. Each of these choices really does go to constitute the very person who will make each subsequent choice. So the possibility of repentance, i.e. of a subsequent choice genuinely incompatible with some previous choice, manifests a lack of integration in the human personality—a lack of integration that we can perhaps understand somewhat in terms of the incomplete integration between our practical *understanding* and our emotions, feelings and drives towards experience. We have no reason to anticipate that the mode in which we might survive—or be resurrected—after death would be a mode of life involving this lack of integration. We have, in other words, no reason to anticipate that we could, after death, reform ourselves by free choices to repent of the choices we made and had not repented before death.

In the second place, analysis of immoral choices indicates how such choices could have lasting significance for one's relationship to God and one's fellows. By 'immoral choice' I mean a free choice to reject integral human fulfilment as identified according to the requirements of practical reasonableness, in favour of some attractive good, participation in which promises me some experience which I choose in preference to what I know to be the reasonable (right, for me in my situation) participation in good. A choice with the same content as this immoral choice may be made by someone who rationalizes it, persuading himself that it is actually no violation of true good, perhaps because (he says to himself) there are no true goods or objective requirements of practical reasonableness; or perhaps because this choice is necessary for the securing of a better proportion (as he supposes) of overall net good in the long run. Sceptical and proportionalist rationalizations are not themselves violations of friendship with the God who favours integral human good. But since they *are* rationalizations, the human intelligence that constructs them can also criticize them. And such a criticism will leave the critic, as chooser, confronted with the possibility of making an immoral choice of the sort I have just defined—a choice known to be unfair, or lying, or unfaithful, or fickle, or arbitrarily self-preferential, or directly destructive of basic human good in myself or in (an)other person(s), or an option for mere appearances instead of reality . . . Such a choice could be known also to be incompatible with friendship with the God who (I am now supposing) has been revealed to favour the human goods we identify in our practical undertanding and remain integrally open to by our reasonable choices.

Plato and Aristotle have left us awesome portraits of the effect on human character of choices known to be immoral in the sense defined above.[6] Such choices are motivated by love of my associates and/or myself, but end in destruction of all human friendships and in loathing for the self that has so preferred inadequate goods, including the cunning of unreasonableness, to the integral participation in human good made possible by fidelity to practical reasonableness. And this self-loathing still does not inspire repentance, because this person has effected a partial but concentrated integration of his character around some set of experiences—say, of domination, or sensual pleasures.

It is not too difficult to envisage, then, the constitution by free choices of a character that would be described simply as repudiating all friendship with God. (The repudiation need not be explicit, and need not be accompanied by the dramatic psychological manifestations portrayed by Plato.) The possibility of having constituted oneself *thus*, at the time of one's death, is the possibility of being in the situation which those who offer to transmit the divine self-disclosure to us have called hell. No-one who has thought seriously about ethics, and about his own character, will be inclined to shrug off the possibility that that is the situation he is heading for because he has already, implicitly, chosen it, or might tomorrow do so.

NOTES

VI.1

Rationality norms . . . See Joseph M. Boyle, Jr., Germain Grisez and Olaf Tollefsen, *Free Choice: A Self-Referential Argument* (University of Notre Dame Press, Notre Dame and London: 1976), pp. 144-52. The whole argument of VI.1 above, for vindicating the existence of free choice, is indebted to Boyle, Grisez and Tollefsen, ibid., and pp. 153-85. See also Finnis, *Natural Law and Natural Rights*, pp. 32-3, 68-9, 385-8.

The history of the identification of free choice . . . See *Ecclesiasticus* 15: 14 with *Deuteronomy* 30: 19; Eric Osborne, *The Beginning of Christian Philosophy* (CUP: 1981), pp. 93-7.

[6] *Republic* IX, 571a-580c; *Nic. Eth.* IX, 4: 1166b4-27.

Choices last . . . See Grisez, *The Way of the Lord Jesus*, chap. 2; Karol Wojtyla, *The Acting Person*, p. 151; also pp. 13, 99, 160. Contrast Hume, *Treatise of Human Nature*, Book II, Part ii, sec. 2: 'Actions are by their very nature temporary and perishing; and where they proceed not from some cause in the character and disposition of the person, who perform'd them, they infix not themselves upon him, and can neither redound to his honour, if good, nor infamy, if evil . . .'

'Choice is determined by our system of preferences' . . . For this characteristic modern denial (equivalently) of free choice, see Hare, *Moral Thinking*, p. 225.

Self-constitution is a necessary effect of one's choice, but typically not a motivating reason . . . Both these points are forcibly made in Wojtyla, *The Acting Person*, pp. 108-9. See also Bernard Williams, *Moral Luck* (CUP: 1981), pp. 50-1; J. L. Stocks, *Morality and Purpose* (ed. D. Z. Phillips, London: 1969), p. 78 (in the article first published as 'Is there a Moral End?', in 1928); J. H. Muirhead, *Rule and End in Morals* (OUP, London: 1932), pp. 55, 88, 109-11.

VI.2

Anscombe on the first person . . . See also Norman Malcolm, 'Whether "I" is a Referring Expression', in Diamond and Teichman (eds.) *Intention and Intentionality: Essays in Honour of G. E. M. Anscombe* (Harvester Press, Brighton: 1979), pp. 15-24.

VI.3

The divine in the ethics of Plato and Aristotle . . . See further *Natural Law and Natural Rights*, pp. 393-8.

Eternal law, the problem of evil, friendship with God . . . On these and other themes of this section, see *Natural Law and Natural Rights*, chap. XIII; Germain Grisez, *Beyond the New Theism: A Philosophy of Religion* (Notre Dame UP, Notre Dame and London: 1975).

VI.4

The paradox of repentance . . . See Geach, *Providence and Evil*, p. 91.

Self-integration and the (im)possibility of repentance after death . . . See Grisez, *The Way of the Lord Jesus*, chap 18.

Index

abortion, 96, 113
act, actuation, actualization
—— knowledge of, as source of knowledge of capacity and nature, 21-2, 25, 51
action, agency, human activity
—— creativity of human and divine a., 146
—— defined, 4
—— direction of, not symmetrical, 116-7
—— 'imperfect a.', 112
—— (in)transitivity of, 10, 139-40, 144, 146
—— as its own point or good, 38-9, 48, 52, 54
—— point of, need not be good consequences, 129
—— 'value of' v. 'value of consequences', 83, 113
—— other references, 1, 4, 33, 37, 51, 147
Adler, Mortimer, 13-15, 17
admirable (morally) (*to kalon*), 7-8
Allan, D.J., 68
analogy, analogical terms, 11
Anscombe, G.E.M.
—— attempted computation of overall net good, 107
—— on consequentialism, 82
—— on ends of human life, 45
—— on first-person, 23, 142, 153
—— on practical knowledge, 2
—— on starting-points of practical reasoning, 31, 35, 45
—— on will and emotion, 54
'anthropocentric categories', 65, 145
anthropology, 3, 51, 63-4, 76-7, 79, 138
—— metaphysical a., 4, 10, 138, *see also* metaphysics
appearance v. reality, 40-1, 48, 52, 75-6, 151
appetite, 43-4, 47
Aquinas, Thomas
—— epistemological principle (from

objects to acts to capacities to nature), 21, 25
—— ethical theory of, 66
—— on analogy, 12
—— on basic forms of human good (ends of human life), 25, 68-9
—— on common good, 131
—— on Eternal Law, 150
—— on good(s), 25, 68
—— on killing, 85, 131
—— on knowledge of human nature, 12, 21
—— on murder, 85, 131
—— on objects of will, 25, 68
—— on practical character of ethics, 24
—— on practical understanding, 11
—— on proportion of means to end, 85
—— on *prudentia*, practical wisdom, 69-70
—— on punishment, 135
—— on self-defence, 85
—— on starting point(s) of practical reasoning, 31, 53, 68
—— on virtue, 12, 69
—— other references, 32, 125
Aristotle
—— anthropology, 12, 21
—— epistemological principle (from objects to acts to capacities to nature), 21, 25, 55
—— fallacious argument(s) from peculiar function or peculiar capacity, 13, 15-16, 17, 24, 71, 122
—— on activity as its own point, 39, 54
—— on character of immoral person, 152
—— on commonsense or common opinion, 17-19, 25, 38-9
—— on deliberation concerning ends, 37, 60, 67-8
—— on ethics, 1, 4, 6-7, 8, 13, 14-15, 17, 20-1, 23, 24

Aristotle (*cont.*)
— on *eudaimonia*, 13, 15, 38, 68
— on free choice, 138
— on friendship with God, 146-7
— on good as object of desire,
    44
— on identity as a good, 39-40
— on nature(s) or essence(s), 21
— on opinions of the multitude,
    17-18
— on 'parts' of intellect, 10-11
— on *phronesis*, 24
— on physics, 14
— on practical intellect, 10, 37
— on practical knowledge, 1, 12,
    14
— on practical reasoning and
    wanting, 31, 37, 53, 60-1, 67-8
— on right by nature, 7, 10, 22,
    24
— on 'seeing' in ethics, 67
— on Socrates' principle, 113
— on the *spoudaios*, 24
— on supreme or ultimate good,
    13, 14, 15, 18, 68
— on *telos* of human existence,
    13-15, 68
— on truth, 24
— on will and reason, 55
— other references, 26, 48, 61,
    124, 153
Aristotelian(ism), neo-Aristotelian,
    12-13, 14, 31, 32, 39, 68, 84
'association of goods', 87, 100-1,
    103-4, 134
Augustine of Hippo, St., 125, 150
authenticity, 47, 48, 50, 52, 70, 73,
    see also identity
autonomy, 122, 124, 139
— intrinsic point of, 124

Bentham, Jeremy, 88
Bergström, Lars, 134
'better', 120
Bible
    — *Deuteronomy* (30:19), 152
    — *Ecclesiasticus* (15:14), 152
    — *John* (11:50), 9, 110
        (18:14), 9, 110
    — *Romans* (3:8), 109, 110-12
        (6:1, 15), 109, 110
Boyle, Joseph M. Jr., 152
Brentano, Franz, 32, 53
Brock, Dan W., 134
Broglie, G. de, 133

Caiaphas 9, 95, 99, 105
capacity, 11, 20
    — known by knowing act(ualiz-
        ation), 21-2, 25, 51
capital punishment, 130, 135
categorical imperative(s), 149 *and see*
    Kant
Catholic(ism), 50, 69, 81-2, 94,
    106-7, 110-11, 138, *see also*
    Vatican II
chance, *see* fortune
character, 6, 10, 40, 119, 139, 140,
    142, 144, 152, *see also* virtue
child, living as, 18, 38   .
choice, (*see also* free choice), 4, 5, 6,
    8, 10, 56, 70, 74, 78, 82, 89,
    117, 119, 120-1, 125, 126,
    143, 151, 153
    — as adoption of one's own
        proposal, 97
    — immoral, defined, 151
    — one's own c., misconstrued as
        one event among others,
        113-4, *and see* eventism
    — serious, aware and deliberate
        c. is a fundamental option,
        144
    — under a description, 45
choosing, 142, *see also* choice
Cicero, 88, 90
'clean hands . . .', 116-17, 142
Clark, Stephen R.L., 39
commitment(s), 66, 75, 77-8, 90-2,
    107, 126, 137, 139, 141
common good, 75, 97, 131, 133,
    149, 150
communities, 75, 121, 128, 131-2,
    144, 147 *and see* friendship
'conflict situations', 93, 102, *see also*
    hard cases
conscience, 71-2, 75, 79
consequences
    — action as first consequence of
        decision, 83
    — reason requires attention to,
        75, 84
    — 'value of c.' v. 'value of act', 83
consequentialism (*see also* proportion-
    alism, utilitarianism)
    — 8, 9, 10, 75, 80, 85-6, 99,
        101-2, 104, 107, 111, 113,
        127, 128-9, 131, 133
    — defined 82-3
consistency, 141
constancy, inconstancy, 75, 90, 91, 151

contemplation, 1, 2, 15, 38, 45
contingency, 126, 136
contrition, 140
convention, 7, 23, 24, 95, 136
Cooper, John M., 23, 54
co-operation, 45, 46-7, 49
cost-benefit analysis, 90-3, 134
courage, 5, 7, 8, 28, 117
creativity, 75, 91
—— of free choice, 138-44, 146
—— of God, 145-7, 149-50
culpability, 143-4

death, 150-2
Decalogue, 69
deliberation, 67-8, 120, 141, see also
    Aristotle, choice, practical
    reasoning
'degrading', 113, 120
demiurgic viewpoint, 11, 111,
    118-20, 126
Democritus of Abdera, 109
'deontological ethics', 84
description, 22
—— action under a, 34-5, 46, 55
—— wanting and choosing under
    a, 45
desirable, 35, 51
desirability characterization, 25,
    34-5, 45
desire(s), 6, 23, 29, 30-7, 42-5, 47,
    54, 58, 63, 77, 82, 123
—— for knowledge or virtue, 43
destiny, human, 10, 133, ch. VI
determinism, 88, 107, 126, 139, 153
deterrence, 128-31 and see terror
    bombing
Dewan, L., 25
disposition, 140
direct choosing against basic good,
    90, 91, 122, 126, 128, 129,
    132-3, 134, see also respect
    for basic goods
Donagan, Alan, 79, 99, 107, 122-3,
    134
'double effect', 85, 132
Dreyfus case, 99
dualism, 61, 123, 125, 134-5
duress, 143
duty, 84, 123

Edgley, Roy, 23
emotion (see also feeling(s)), 47-8,
    53, 73, 75
empiricism, 42-3, 51, 52, 64, 123

end
—— defined, 122
—— does not justify means,
    109-10
—— 'must not be contradicted by
    means', 100, 102, 108
—— intelligible, 122-3
ends, of human action, existence, life,
    21, 36-7, 45, 68, 84, and see
    goods, basic
Enlightenment, 138
essence (nature), known by knowing
    act(ualization), 21, 25
Eternal Law, 150, 153
ethics
—— as activity, 1-6, 20
—— as deontological and teleo-
    logical, 84
—— as a foundation of knowledge
    of human nature, 21-2, 40,
    71, 137
—— as practical reasonableness,
    137
—— as theory, 2-3, 4, 5, 19
—— dependence on knowledge of
    human nature, 22
—— master (most general) prin-
    ciple of, 70, 72, 76, 120-1,
    124, 127, 151-2
—— object(ive)s of, 3-4, 10, 18,
    20, 21, 94
—— objectivity of, 10, 22, ch. III
—— philosophical e., 69-71, 146
—— practical character of, 1-6,
    10, 18, 24, 50, 117
—— (great) questions of, 6, 9, 95,
    105
—— source of, 56
—— subject-matter of, 1, 3, 5, 7,
    9, 18, 21, 50
eudaimonia, 8, 13, 15, 19, 38, 68
eupraxia, 8
euthanasia, 106-7
evaluation, 22
'eventism', 72, 113-20
evil(s), 87, 103, 110-11, 149-50, 153
—— 'doing evil', 'evil act', 112
'exception-making', 127, 143
experience(s), 48
—— agreeable, attractive or wel-
    come as satisfying, 9, 23, 36,
    42, 47-8, 151-2
—— as passive, 38
—— pre-philosophic, 18-19, 25,
    137-8

experience(s) (*cont.*),
— — inter-subjectively knowable,
    61
'experience machine', 36-42, 46, 48,
    50, 52, 75, 89, 123
extenuating circumstances, 143-4
extortion, 98, 100, 103

fair(ness), unfairness, 90, 109, 128-9,
    132
fanaticism, 90, 102
feeling(s), 32-5, 38, 41, 46-8, 53, 63,
    73, 126
Feinberg, Joel, 108
Finnis, J.M., 10, 22, 23, 24, 25, 50-1,
    53, 55, 60, 75, 79, 84, 106-7,
    127, 134, 145-6, 152-3
first-person, *see also* transparency
— — perspective, 114, 116-8, 134
— — statements, 3, 71
flourishing, 8, 21, 38, 50, 52, 60, 68,
    72, 74, 122, 124, 148
Foot, Philippa, 28-9, 49, 62-3
fortune (chance, fate, luck, favourable
    circumstances), 8, 20, 48, 136,
    147, *see also* contingency
free choice (*see also* choice), 10, 40,
    47, 88, 149, 150, 152
— — defined, 137, 138
— — existence of, vindicated,
    137-8
— — experience of, 6, 137-8
— — good of, 128
— — lastingness of, 6, 40, 139-44,
    153
— — participation in goods
    through, 74, 150
— — prestige of, 82
— — significance of, 136-42
— — transitivity and intransitivity
    of, 10, 139-40, 144, 146
friendship, 51, 124, 144, 146
— — defined, 147-8
— — with God, 148-52, 153
fulfil(ment), 17, 20, 37-8, 121, 151,
    see also flourishing, perfection
'fundamental option', 142-4

Gauthier, R.A., 68
Geach, P.T., 49, 107, 134, 153
givenness, of human existence, 40
God, 110-11, 124, 146-52
good(s)
— — basic (forms of human g.), 5,
    22, 44, 50-1, 53, 54, 66, 68-9,
    70, 74, 76-7, 81, 84, 89, 91,
    124, 125
— — conception that it would be
    good to . . ., 33-4, 45
— — emotion as aspect of, 47-8
— — fundamental sense of, 7, 8, 9,
    11-12
— — intelligible, 42-5, 74, 138, 143
— — orderliness and beauty of, 147
— — participation in, *see* partici-
    pation
— — 'pre-moral', 112
— — respect for basic goods, 122-7,
    see also respect
— — thin theories of, 48-50, 81-2,
    124
— — understood, 33-4, 42, 44-5,
    47-8, 54, 73, 123, 141
— — as fulfilment, 12
— — as the perfecting, 44, 54, 72
— — as satisfactoriness, 31
— — as what it is intelligent to take
    a practical interest in, 62
— — of knowledge (truth), 2-4, 52
— — 'of order', 43-5
— — of practical reasonableness,
    52, 69, 70-4
— — of universe, 145, 147, 150
gratitude, 129
Grisez, Germain, vii, 76, 79, 108, 135,
    152-3
Grover, Robinson A., 88

habit(s), 138-40
happiness, 8, 81, 123-4, 125
hard cases, 83, 95, *see also* conflict
    situations
Hare, R.M., 88, 95, 96, 98, 104-5,
    106, 119, 135, 153
harm, 36, 86, 87, 105, 108, 114, 116,
    130-1
hatred, 36, 76
hell, 152
heteronomy, 124
Hill, Thomas E. Jr., 134
Hobbes, Thomas, 26, 28, 29, 32,
    49-50, 55, 60, 64
humanity
— — basic goods intrinsic to, 125
— — insulting h., 104
— — Kant's restricted sense of,
    122-4, 134
— — respect for in every action
    (not treating as a mere means),
    121-4, 132, 134

Hume, David, 7, 26-7, 28, 32, 44,
    47, 49, 57-8, 64-5, 78, 153
Humean, neo-Humean, 14, 29, 31,
    44, 60-1, 122, 124

identity, value of preserving one's, 19,
    39-40, see also authenticity
immoral choice, defined, 151
'imperfect act', 112
inclination(s), 32, 34, 46-7, 51, 73-4,
    123-4, 140
incommensurability, of basic goods,
    66, 86-93, 99, 107, 108, 119,
    120, 126, 138
innocent, killing or harming of, 9, 96,
    104, 105, 116, 127-32, 136
inquiry, 2, 4-5, see also theory, truth
integration, 73, 151-2, see also self-
    integration
intelligence, 11, 42, 45, 47-8, 55, 71,
    77
— and intelligibility, 36, 136
intention, 116, 117-8, 129, 131, 132
'intermediate principles' of morality
    (or requirements of practical
    reasonableness), 69-70, 74-6,
    84, 93, 121, 124
interest(s), 62-3
intransitivity, see free choice
intuition, 4, 51, 59, 104, 125-6
intuitionism, 22
involuntary acts, 131, 132
irrational(ity), 28-30, 52-3
'is' and 'ought', 10

James, William, 81-2, 106
Janssens, Louis, 100, 102
Jesuits, 38
Judaism, 110-11
judgment, 42
just(ice), 6-7, 8, 9, 113, 128-33, 142

Kant, Immanuel
— misunderstanding of practical
    reasonableness, 122-3, 134
— on categorical imperative(s),
    75, 120-1, 123
— on good will, 73-4, 125
— on treating humanity as an
    end, 109, 121-4, 127, 134
— on proportionalism, 120, 125
— methodology of, 122
— on happiness, 123
— other references, 70, 75
Kantianism, 108, 134-5

'Kantian principles', 109, 120-4,
    125-7
— defined, 125
Kenny, Anthony, 25, 30-2, 35, 44
    killing, when justifiable, 130-3
Knauer, Peter, 108
knowledge, see also practical knowl-
    edge, truth
— 2, 51, 52, 60, 140, 146
— anthropocentric, 65

language, 18, 28, see also meaning
legalism, 77-8, 93-4
Leon of Salamis, 113, 115-6, 119,
    139, 142-3
lesser evil, 'principle of', 90, 93, 99,
    107-8, 111, 126, 133
liberty (see also free choice),
— good of, 50, 128
life, good of, 40, 46, see also killing,
    murder
'life-plan', 46, 49
Linacre Centre (Euthanasia and
    Clinical Practice), 107, 108
Locke, John, 58, 65, 78
Lonergan, Bernard J.F., 21, 32,
    42-5, 49, 54
love, 149-50, 152, see also friendship

Mackie, J.L., 26-7, 57-9, 64, 76, 78
McCormick, Richard A., 93, 95, 96,
    98-104, 106, 112, 127-8, 131,
    142
McDowell, John, 20, 28-9, 52-3, 68,
    78
Malcolm, Norman, 153
master principle, see ethics, principle
meaning, 58-9, 63-4
meta-ethics, 4, 5, 18, 27-8
metaphysics, 10, 40, 71, 138, see also
    anthropology
Mill, John Stuart, 50, 55
Model Penal Code, 97
Monan, J. Donald, 25
moral(ity), 6, 7, 8, 12, 53
— incorporates Socrates' prin-
    ciple, 116
— m. good, 53, 125
— m. choice (i.e. deliberate
    choice), 136
— m. evil, 112
— m. philosophy, 6, 70
— m. precepts, principles, norms,
    rules, 56-7, 69-70, 74-8, 84
— m. problems, 92-3

moral(ity) (*cont.*),
— m. statements, 27
— m. wrong, 89, 151
motivation, 35, 48, 141-2, 153
Muirhead, J.H., 153
Müller, Anselm W., 114, 116-9, 134
murder, 96, 103, 107, 113, 120,
    143
— defined, 104

Nagel, Thomas, 29, 61-2, 143
natural
— as fulfilling, 17, 20
— n. law, n. reason, 68-9, 110,
    130
— science(s), 42, 61-2, 138, 140,
    see also scientism
nature
— human, 4, 10, 12, 17, 20, 40,
    48, 52, 122-4
— v. convention, 7, 10
— knowledge of human n., how
    acquired, 20-2, 25, 137-8
— as 'of that sort', 12
— 'follow n.', as ethical norm,
    124, 134-5
'necessity', 126, 143
negligence, 128
Nietzsche, Friedrich, 7
Nirvana, 50
Nozick, Robert, 38-41

object(s) (objective of . . .)
— knowledge of, as source of
    knowledge of nature, 21-2,
    25, 51
— of action, 45
— of desire, 44
— of inclination, 51, 74
— of ethics, 3-4
— of human life, 21, 35
— of practical reasoning, 31, 35
— of theory, 2
— of will, 25, 68
'objectification', 'projection', 27, 58,
    65-6
objective,
— o. goodness of states of affairs,
    29, 62
— o. probabilities, 107
— o. relationships, 61-2
— 'o. standpoint' (*see also*
    eventism), 61, 118-9
— v. subjectivity, 61-3
objectivity, 63

— of persons, agents, 56, 60-1, ,
    77
— of judgments, 7, 10, 22-3, 24,
    53, 56, 59-60, 63, 66-7, 77
O'Connell, Timothy, 88, 95
opportunity, 34, 50-1, 56, 70, 75,
    124, 137, 143, 146
optimizing, 82-3, 87, 92
order, good of, 43-5, 46
ordinal v. cardinal computations, 87,
    91, 92
Osborne, Eric, 152
outcomes, results, 112, 113, 118,
    136-7, 139, *see also* states of
    affairs

pain, 82, 88
participation, in good(s), 3, 4, 5, 21,
    22, 36, 44, 47-8, 70, 72, 120,
    144, 149, 150, 151-2
— defined, 46
passion(s), 48-9, 123
Paul, St., Pauline principle, 75,
    109-11, 121, 124
perfection(s), imperfection, 44, 54,
    72, 112, 123-4, 125
person(s), 89, 125, 126-7, 139-42, 146
philosophy (*see also* ethics, moral
    philosophy), 19, 42, 69, 146,
    150
Pinckaers, Servais, 106
Plato (*see also* Socrates), 26, 38, 48,
    84, 109, 112-3, 114, 124, 153
— on appearance v. reality, 40-1
— on desire and good, 44
— on divine play, 148, 153
— on free choice, 138
— on good of justice/morality,
    8, 113, 152
— on scepticism, 7
play, 51, 70, 148-9
pleasure, 37, 81, 82, 88-9
potentiality, power, *see* capacity
Pound, Roscoe, 81, 106
practical
— defined, 3, 10, 11, 12
— disciples, 77
— intelligence, 45-6
— judgment(s), 78, 133, 141
— knowledge, 2, 146
— propositions, 141
— reason, 2, 21, 35, 44, 48, 68,
    111, 117
— reasonableness, *see* reasonable-
    ness

— — reasoning, 35, 51, 53, 118-9,
    124, 137-8
— — truth, 67
— — understanding, 4-5, 10,
    11-12, 34-5, 44, 51, 74, 138,
    151
— — wisdom, 69-70
praise, 129
praxis, 1, 138
preference(s), 81-2, 106, 128, 138,
    139
'pre-moral good and evil', 112
prescriptivism, 28, 70
principle(s)
— — basic or first principles of
    practical reasoning, 44, 68-9,
    84, 91 *and see* goods, basic
— — intermediate principles of
    practical reasoning (methodo-
    logical requirements of prac-
    tical reasonableness), 69-70,
    74-6, 84, 90, 91, 138, 141
— — master, i.e. most general,
    (intermediate) moral principle,
    70, 72, 76, 120-1, 124, 127,
    151-2
— — concrete moral principles,
    norms, rules, 56-7, 70, 74, 78,
    84, 141
— — other references, 9, 110, 120,
    138, 141, 148
Prior, A.N., 88, 107
'projection', *see* objectification
proportionalism (*see also* consequen-
    tialism, utilitarianism)
— — 8, 9, 10, 80, 92, 121, 131,
    132, 133, 136-7, 151
— — defined, 85-7
— — always rationalization, 94,
    136
— — cannot accomodate Socrates'
    principle, 112-20
— — eliminates common sense dis-
    tinctions, 112
— — eventist character of, 112-20
— — imaginary demiurgic perspec-
    tive of, 111, 118-20, 126
— — imposes impossible respons-
    ibility, 136
— — irrational, 87-90, 91-2
— — logically ineligible to guide
    practical reasoning, 120
— — mislocates wrong, 105
— — (new) theological form of, 98,
    99-104, 133-4

— — not coherent with Judaeo-
    Christian belief in providence,
    110-11, 133
— — undermines respect for
    human good, 125
proportion(ality), non-proportionalist
    references to, 85, 86, 106-7,
    132
providence, 110-11, 146-50
public officer, 128, 130-2
punishment, 116, 128-33

queerness, argument for scepticism
    from, 57-60

Rahner, Karl, 134-5
rationality norms, 137, 138, 152
rationalization, 9, 77, 83, 94-9, 100,
    104-5, 120, 126, 136, 143,
    151
Rawls, John, 13, 48-9, 81-2
Raz, Joseph, 134
reality v. appearance, *see* appear-
    ance
reason, 28-9
— — and will, 47, 54
— — for action, 29
— — 'proportionate', 102, *see also*
    proportionalism
— — 'right reason', *see recta ratio*
— — v. passions, 48, 49, 73, 76,
    123
reasonableness (practical), 5, 22, 53,
    99, 144, 146
— — and ethics, 137
— — architectonic, 72-4
— — good of, 52, 69, 70, 120, 124
— — master or most general prin-
    ciple of, 70, 72, 76, 120-1,
    124, 127, 151-2
— — requirements of, 22, 53, 56,
    75-8, 84, 90-1, 126, 151
— — transparent for the other
    goods, 70-4, 120, 124, 152
recta ratio, 72-3, *see also* reasonable-
    ness
reductivism, 4, 26-30, 52, 64, 66
reflection, 51-2
reform, 140, 142
Reformation, 138
regret, 139, 142, 143
relativity, argument for scepticism
    from, 57, 74-8
repentance, 40, 119, 139-40, 142,
    150-2, 153

respect
—— for basic goods, 122-7, 129, 149
—— for humanity, 121-4
—— for persons, 125, 126, 127, 129, 142
responsibility, 98-9, 107, 111, 125-7, 132-3, 136, 149-50
results, see outcomes
retribution, 128-30
revelation, 69, 110, 146-7, 150
right
—— and wrong, 58, 67, 77, 83-4, 89, 111, 113, see also conscience, moral(ity)
—— unique r. answer, 70, 77-8, 93-4, 134
rights, 103, 127, 129, 136
ripple in pond postulate, 98-9, 119
Rule of Law, 139
Russell, Bertrand, 81, 106

satisfaction(s), 6, 9, 31, 36, 37, 42, 43-4, 73, 105, 147
satisfactoriness, 31
scepticism, 7, 10, 26, 28, 53, 56-60, 76-7, 79, 80, 136-7, 151
Scheler, Max, 32, 53-4
Schüller, Bruno, 88, 95, 96-9, 106
science, see natural science
scientism, 61-2, 78
'self', 61, 124, 142-4
self-consciousness, 142
self-constitution, self-creation, self-determination, 3, 6, 40, 72, 124, 138-44, 150-2, 153
self-cultivation, 121, 148-9
'self-contradiction'
—— alleged by new proportionalists, 100, 103, 108
—— in choice, 115, 119, 141
self-deception, 141
self-defence, 116, 132-3
self-integration, 142, 144, 153
self-interest(s), 8-9
selfishness, 142-3
self-loathing, 152
self-love, 148-9, 152
self-refutation, 5, 23, 56, 59, 60, 137, 138
self-perfection, 149
self-preference, 121, 128, 151
sentiments, 27-8
sex, 6, 8

Sextus Empiricus, 79
side-constraints, 121
simulation, see appearance
sin, 71-2, 110-11, and see wrong
Smart, J.J.C., 95, 98, 107
Socrates, Socrates' principle, 7, 8, 9, 109, 112-16, 118-9, 124, 139, 142
Solzhenitsyn, Alexander, 117
'speculative' intelligence, knowledge, understanding (see also theory), 2, 11, 117
spirit, 140, 141
states of affairs,
—— evaluation of, 62, 89, 90, 113-4, 116-20, 121, 122-3, 125, 129, 133
—— existence and explanation of, 145-6
—— as transitive results of choice, 139
Stocks, J.L., 153
Suarezian (ideas of Francisco Suarez), 124, 134-5
'subjective standpoint', 118, see also eventism
subjectivity
—— of merely relative to us, 145, 150
—— v. objectivity, see objectivity
subsidiarity, 38-9
suicide, 39-40, 107, 113, 127, 134
Summers, R.S., 106
sympathy, 125
synderesis, 32

Tarski, Alfred, 63
'teleological ethics', 80, 84-5, 106
terror bombing, 96, 103, 133
theoretical v. practical, 2, 4, 10-11, 14, 15, 22, 60
theory (see also inquiry), 1-3, 5, 11, 59
Thirty Commissioners (Tyrants of Athens), 112-3, 115-7
Thomists, 32, 44, 84
thought-experiment
—— the experience machine, 36-42, 46, 48, 50, 52, 75, 89, 123
—— the sheriff, 95-9, 100-3, 129
Thucydides, 7, 26
transitive effects of choice, see free choice
translation, 63-4

transparency, 3, 23, 70-4, 79, 114,
   117, 141, 143, 149
truth (see also knowledge), 58, 63-6
   —— as good, 2, 4, 6, 11, 56, 60
   —— as object of inquiry, 2-4, 11,
      64, 137

uncaused causing, 145
underdetermination, cognitive, 78
understanding (see also practical
   understanding), 34, 37, 42, 44,
   46, 51, 54, 74, 140
universalizing, 28, 70, 74, 97, 121,
   125, 139, 140-1
universe, order and good of, 144-5,
   150
utilitarianism (see also consequentialism, proportionalism)
   —— 8, 9, 10, 37, 70, 75, 83, 85-6,
      95, 98-9, 104, 106, 120, 128-9
   —— defined, 80-2
   —— preference u., 81-2, 106
utility, 73, 80-1, 86, 107

value(s), see good
variety of moral beliefs, see relativity
Vatican II, Second V. Council, 50,
   55, 113, 120

Veatch, Henry, 13-17, 18-19, 20
vice(s), 113, 140
virtue(s), 5-6, 49, 53, 57, 69, 113,
   140, 144, 148
   —— defined, 56
Voegelin, Eric, 24, 79

'wants', 138
   —— v. 'things wanted', 31, 35,
      44-5
Wechsler, Herbert, 97
well-being, see good
Wiggins, David, 29, 63-7, 68, 78, 79
will, 55, 73, 123
   —— defined, 47, 139
Williams, Bernard, 153
wishful thinking, 141
Wojtyla, Karol, 54, 153
wrong (see also right and wrong), 53,
   144
   —— can be deliberately chosen,
      111
   —— mislocated by proportionalists
      and utilitarians, 89, 103-5, 134
   —— never to be chosen, 116-7
   —— suffering w. better than doing
      w., 7-8, 9, 105, 109, 112-20
wrongdoer, 116-7